Epping Forest from a transparency:
by courtesy of Bernard Ward

HENRY DOUBLEDAY
THE EPPING NATURALIST

HENRY DOUBLEDAY

The Epping Naturalist

ROBERT MAYS

Fellow of the Royal Entomological Society

FOREWORD BY SIR WILLIAM ADDISON

1978
PRECISION PRESS

First published in 1978

Precision Press
15 High Street
Marlow Bucks

ISBN 0 9500638 4 3

PRINTED IN GREAT BRITAIN
BY PRECISION PRESS, MARLOW, BUCKS

CONTENTS

FOREWORD

Those who are studiously inclined today may learn either more-
and-more about less-and-less or less-and-less about more-and-more.
In the 19th century the choice seldom existed. Few could afford to
travel in search of new experiences or cultivate their minds through
a multitude of expensive pastimes. But what was lost in breadth was
frequently gained in depth. This book is a reminder of what a man
of modest means, utterly devoid of personal ambition, could
achieve a hundred years ago by single-minded dedication to one
consuming interest. It may even cause some readers to pause and
ask whether we are not now in danger of equating our much vaunted
rise in the standard of living with the mere proliferation of trivia.

The Epping naturalist, Henry Doubleday, was the son of a
Quaker grocer and lived out his life in the quiet environment of
shop, countryside and meeting-house into which he had been born.
The shop was within a stone's throw of the meeting-house, Isaac
Payne's Quaker school was within a stone's throw of either, and the
countryside surrounded them. It was a small world: but what of it?
Robert Mays does well to quote a sentence from Arthur Raistrick's
Quakers in Science and Industry: 'In search for innocent trades
they [the Quakers] virtually discovered a new world . . . the world
of domestic market for humble everyday articles.' A score of
nationally known trade-names must spring to mind, associated with
Quaker tradesmen who from humble beginnings rose to wealth
and renown by industry and fair dealing. In Essex the Henry Doubleday Research Association at Bocking reminds us of the Coggleshall
Doubledays, who made their mark as seedsmen and market garden-
ers. Their cousins at Epping lacked this flair for commercial success;
but whether lived in simple dignity by Cumbrian 'statesmen',
Yorkshire chocolate manufacturers, or Essex grocers and seedsmen,
the Quaker way of life varied little, and we have evidence of its
quality in the diaries of Susanna Day, wife of a Quaker grocer of
Saffron Walden, whose business must have been practically identical
with that of Henry's more prosperous father, Benjamin Doubleday
of Epping. The Days had as shop assistants and members of their
household such young men as Robert Lloyd, the Quaker poet and
friend of Charles Lamb, and Thomas Rickman, who gave the
names by which they are still known to our distinctive styles of
architecture. Henry Doubleday, who inherited his father's business,

had James English, the son of a local gardener who became a skilful taxidermist and a founder-member of the Essex Field Club.

To the Doubleday grocery store in Henry's time came naturalists from remote parts of England and even from overseas; but inevitably the most regular visitors were members of that remarkable group of naturalists, most of them Quakers at that time, who made Epping Forest their special field of study: the Forster brothers, Edward Newman, and their friends and neighbours. From time to time they would be joined by George Stacey Gibson, the Saffron Walden banker, to whose *Flora of Essex* Doubleday contributed a list of plants found in Epping Forest. Conversation on such occasions may not have promoted the sale of grocery; but it would have done credit to any college common room.

We have waited a long time for this book. When Robert Mays read a paper on Henry Doubleday to the Essex Field Club eighteen years ago it was already clear that he was well qualified by knowledge and sympathy to write as full-scale a memoir as was ever likely to be possible of a subject so self-effacing. Even modesty can be carried to excess! At Henry Doubleday's death Edward Newman wrote: 'With him has died a larger amount of natural history knowledge than has ever been possessed by any one of our countrymen.' Most of this knowledge was communicated in letters to fellow naturalists who had written to him for information: little apart from the *Synonymic List of British Lepidoptera* had been made available directly to a wider public. He was too shy and self-distrustful to court publicity for his findings.

Unfortunately, the man who was held in honour by such internationally known entomologists as Achille Guenée of France and Baron von Nolcken of Russia was not the man his father had been behind the counter. Towards the end of his life his business affairs became sadly confused, and when the local bank he had entrusted with his savings collapsed he was all but forced into bankruptcy. A nervous breakdown followed, from which he never completely recovered.

Quakers have always set great store on the prompt payment of debts. So when it became known that Henry Doubleday was no longer able to meet the demands of his creditors the Quakers of West Essex—many of whom were well-to-do—rallied to his aid and established a Trust to provide him with modest means of subsistence and save his collection of lepidoptera from dispersal. It is to the three trustees who became his executors, James Hack Tuke, George Stacey Gibson, and Joseph Gurney Barclay, that we owe the preservation of this magnificent collection of moths and butterflies, which is now available to students at South Kensington.

As one who has long revered the memory of Henry Doubleday, and who for more than twenty years has been a Verderer of his beloved Forest, I warmly commend this book. It is particularly appropriate that it should be published in the centenary year of the Epping Forest Act, 1878. Although Henry Doubleday did not live to see the Act passed, he did live to share in the public rejoicing that followed the judgment of the Master of the Rolls, Sir George Jessel, by which Epping Forest was saved for the recreation of the People, and to be the happy hunting ground of naturalists for all time.

WILLIAM ADDISON

Epping

In his search for truth in Natural History and in his life-long study of birds and insects, Henry Doubleday was tireless. He left little positively to identify him in after years, for few publications came from his pen over his own name; but he was a prolific correspondent, and was of great help to other naturalists when compiling material for publication. He was a man who was persistent in following his life's work, forthright in stating his views, courageous in face of physical handicaps.

The excuse for writing this brief biographical sketch is my desire that the record of the work of this 19th Century amateur naturalist, Henry Doubleday, the Epping grocer, should not be overlooked, which the tremendous scientific advances of recent years may easily lead us to do. Doubleday, who was pre-eminent as a British lepidopterist, died just one hundred years ago.

A brief account of his life was published in the *Essex Naturalist* in 1956[1]; this is the Journal of the Essex Field Club, which upon its one thousandth Field Meeting on 8th September 1956 paid homage to Henry Doubleday and to the great botanist John Ray by visiting the former's grave at Epping and by a pilgrimage to Ray's tomb at Black Notley. He was also the subject of a talk given some years ago to the Essex Field Club, an abbreviated account of which was reported in the *Essex Naturalist*.[2]

The derivation of the name Doubleday[3] is obscure; as Lower in his *Patronymica Britanica* (1860) says, 'This name and its companion, Singleday, baffle my ingenuity!' Some 40 years later Bardsley in his *Dictionary of English and Welsh Surnames*[4] explained the name as probably deriving from a nickname 'duble-dent' i.e. double-tooth; it is a name which, said Bardsley, 'troubled Mr. Lower sorely, and over which I myself have spent many a miserable ten minutes'.

Latin names have been largely avoided. The changes in nomenclature during the last 100 years have been so great that the use of many scientific names employed by Doubleday and his contemporaries might now be misleading, although where they have been kept they may not necessarily be those by which naturalists know them today. Many people have kindly lent me letters to peruse, and assisted in other ways; in this connection I must mention particularly the late Thomas Doubleday of Coggeshall, the late Mr. J. Gaze of Castle Hedingham, Mr. A. C. Wheeler of the British Museum

(Natural History), the Librarians of the Essex Field Club, and of the Society of Friends at Friends House, London and Mr. David Wilson for the photographs.

Readers who wish to follow up references will find them in the combined Bibliography and Notes.

Barnards Farm, December 1975.

The Doubleday family coat of arms, granted in 1640

Henry Doubleday, circa 1863

FAMILY BACKGROUND

Early in the 19th Century two Quakers, Benjamin and Mary Doubleday lived in a large brick house[5] situated on the western side of the High Street in Epping, and it was here, on Sunday 1st July 1808[6] their son Henry was born. In later years he was affectionately regarded among Essex naturalists as the doyen of entomologists in that county. The house was known formerly as the Black Boy Inn and was converted into a shop by Benjamin's parents when they settled there some 40 years earlier; a flourishing business in hardware and grocery was built up.

The Doubleday family were Quakers over many generations from the rise of that religious body in the early 17th Century, and they helped build up the Quaker reputation for honest dealing and fair trading during the 18th and 19th Centuries; over the years they were firm in their beliefs and were true to their principles in difficult times, through persecution and in face of ignorant opposition. Arthur Raistrick, in *Quakers in Science and Industry*[7] says 'In search for innocent trades they (Quakers) virtually discovered a new world waiting for conquest, the world of domestic market for humble everyday articles'. In explanation of the 'innocent' trades, it should be stated that in general, any trade was avoided which was at all connected with activities unacceptable to Quakers, which included, for example, the importation of cotton, because of its dependence on slave labour, and, latterly, the brewing trade; further, most professions were closed to them, because of the universities' Oath of Allegiance; so much for the general background of the Quaker attitude towards business, to which the Doubledays adhered: they had found their 'innocent trade'.[8]

THE FOREST

Some three years after the birth of Henry another son, Edward, was born, both brothers as they grew up falling under the spell of the charm of the rural Essex countryside. There were no other children and neither married. Their great delight in their early days was to roam together the neighbourhood of Epping, which is surrounded by an area of heath and woodland; but it was very different in those days, the wilder parts being visited by far fewer people, although frequented by London bird catchers and other collectors; consequently much of the animal life continued there relatively unmolested, indeed, many entomologists considered Epping Forest to be one of the richest hunting grounds in England, and Henry, since he was quite young, had taken a keen interest in the wild life to be found there. Today, of course, the encroachment of building to its boundaries and its attractions, because of easy access for city dwellers, have inevitably caused the Forest to suffer grievously in the disappearance of many of its rarest inhabitants. The extinction or extreme scarcity of many species of insects with which Henry was familiar in his local hunting grounds would have saddened him, but he could have had little idea of the problems of pollution and habitat destruction facing us today: fortunately the effects of these threats to wild life are now more widely appreciated, and greater concern is shown for the elimination of such dangers.

So far as the species of butterflies and moths are concerned, there can be little doubt that, judging by Doubleday's records, they were much more abundant in his time than today, and that this was so even about fifty years after his death, was confirmed by A. W. Mera in an article *Butterflies of Epping Forest*, published in the *Essex Naturalist*[9] at that time, in which the list is very much poorer than Doubleday's, and this was also corroborated by other lepidopterists. Although not far from London however, it is still looked upon favourably by naturalists, and the observant rambler may yet catch sight of the herd of fallow deer which still keeps a precarious foothold in the Forest, or see young badgers at play in the twilight.

The story of how Epping Forest was preserved for everyone to enjoy is a long one and has been told frequently elsewhere; but the facts may be briefly recounted, for Doubleday must have been acutely anxious over the fate of his beloved woodlands, although by the time of his death in 1875 the struggle was virtually over and most of the Forest had been saved. In 1866 the Lord of the Manor of Loughton enclosed about 1,300 acres of Forest land and, without Parliamentary consent, began felling the trees: this action so incensed one Willingale of Loughton, whose livelihood consisted of lopping wood in the Forest, that he, with his two sons, broke down the fences enclosing the Forest land; for this offence they were imprisoned by the local magistrates, at least one of whom was bribed by the Lord of the Manor, and whilst in prison, one son contracted pneumonia and died. The case, which aroused great indignation at the time, was taken up by the Commons Preservation Society, but Willingale himself died in 1870 and the action was consequently dropped. But that was not an end to it, for in 1871 the Corporation of London became involved, and opened up a case against the Lords of the Manors who had by then enclosed no less than 3,000 acres of Epping Forest land. This land was recovered when they won their case in 1874, making a total of 6,000 acres of forest we know today. The enclosures took place between 1851 and 1871, and although the Forest was not entirely thrown open until three years after his death, Doubleday must have known that it would be preserved, and that undoubtedly gave him great joy. Londoners, in particular, must ever be grateful for the courageous action of the Willingales which saved the Forest, action which was undertaken despite the severe obstacles which were put in their way.[10]

Not a great deal of information can be gleaned about the Doubleday brothers' childhood and school-days, but we know that Henry, with his younger brother Edward, attended the popular Quaker school at Epping, Isaac Payne's,[11] and there he received a good classical education which stood him in good stead in after years, his knowledge of Latin being invaluable in his natural history studies.

A schoolfellow, Henry Deane,[12] the son of Quaker parents, Moses and Elizabeth Deane, in describing his own school-days at Isaac Payne's, said he was 'systematically taught and knew the value and pleasure of learning'. Deane, whom Edward Newman, the editor of the *Entomologist*, described as a most painstaking entomologist but unknown as a collector of insects, wrote in high praise of his early school-friends, the Doubleday brothers, 'who,' he said, 'have since attained a world-wide notoriety as entomologists. I was occasionally favoured with an invitation to go home with them to tea, occasions which were highly prized, as affording opportunities for seeing their collections and illustrated books on Natural History. From collecting insects, collecting plants and drying them—without regard to names, but for their intrinsic beauty—seemed naturally to follow. Thus habits of observing the beauties of creative wisdom were early fixed in my heart, and I often look back with thankfulness to that now far distant day when my friends the Doubledays sowed that seed which was to keep out many temptations to evil, and to prove such a lasting source of pure enjoyment.'

A childhood incident in the life of the young Doubledays came to

3

light in 1894 when a local Essex newspaper[13] reported, under the heading '*Interesting Find*', as follows:—'Mr. Joseph Hills, who is having extensive alterations made to his establishments, has a relic of considerable interest which the builder (Mr. Whiffin) found secreted in one of the old chimneys. It was enclosed in a strong old blacking bottle, carefully sealed and consists of a parchment which sets forth that it and nine copper coins were placed there by Henry Doubleday, aged ten years, and Edward Doubleday, aged eight years, sons of Benjamin and Mary Doubleday, on 26th April 1819. It also gives the prices of goods then current, as follows: Flour, 65s per sack; wheat, £18 per load; bread, 1s per quartern loaf; candles, 1s per lb; soap, 11d per lb; cheese, 7d to 1s per lb; and butter 10d to 1/4d.' Although not mentioned in this extract, it is recorded elsewhere[14] that Henry Doubleday also left a memorandum in the blacking bottle reading as follows:—'Scarce any gold in circulation owing to the restriction of the bank, which is prevented by Government from issuing any gold in exchange for their notes, which are as low as 20 shillings. Written on the 26th of fourth month 1819.' A list of the principal inhabitants of Epping was also enclosed.

These notes written at an early age would seem to indicate considerable business acumen, but unfortunately for Henry, when the time came for him to accept full responsibility for the shop management, he was, as will be seen later, extremely unsuccessful, his generous nature and devotion to his chosen leisure studies contributing to a disastrous end to his business career.

LOCAL AND FAMILY CONNECTIONS

We can imagine Henry and his brother Edward locking the shop door and carefully extinguishing the oil lamps to hasten off together to their beloved woods on a summer's evening in search of moths and other insects of the twilight. Henry's unbounded enthusiasm for natural history, not so far as we know, shared by his parents, led more and more frequently to his absence from the shop-counter; life, however, went on pleasantly enough for him until he was forty, and much time was spent collecting birds and insects not only in the neighbouring woodlands but also in the eastern counties of England and, his father being alive, he was not unduly worried about the successful continuation of the family trade; but on Christmas Eve 1847 he suffered a severe blow in the death of his father, which

4

compelled him to carry the burden of the business alone, for his livelihood depended upon it. His brother, who had left home, first travelling abroad and then accepting a post with the British Museum, died tragically early, in 1849,[15] undoubtedly cutting short a brilliant career, which will be touched on later. Two years earlier their mother, Mary Doubleday, had died at the age of sixty-seven. Left to himself Henry managed as well as he could, but it was a great trial and one for which he was in many ways unsuited.

His father, Benjamin, was spoken of as a man of great integrity and it is clear he took a fairly prominent part in Epping affairs, some of which may be gleaned from old records. One of his activities was to act as Treasurer, from 1825, of the Epping and Ongar Highway Trust,[16] which was formed in 1769 and terminated just one hundred years later, its purpose being to control and maintain the roads in the Forest area. It had authority over the Turnpike road from Writtle through Ongar and Epping as far as Woodford Wells, and the short stretch of road from Epping to Harlow Bush Common. The Essex and Hertfordshire Trust had jurisdiction over the Turnpike road from Harlow so far as Stump Cross on the way to Cambridge and Newmarket, and the Middlesex and Essex Trust over the road from Woodford Wells to London.

The Act of Parliament creating the Epping and Ongar Trust transferred the management of the Epping highways from the local magistrates to Trustees. As an example of the Trust's power, they lessened the gradients of Buckhurst Hill and Golden's (Goldings) Hill, and in 1830 commenced making a new road through the heart of the Forest from the Wake Arms Inn to Woodford; appended to this Act was the rather lengthy list of the names of the first appointed Trustees, together with their qualifications, which required *inter alia*, personal estate of £1,000 or a clear £50 per annum from rents; included in this list of the early Trust members was one John Doubleday who was one of certain nominated Trustees appointed to investigate and report on the 'evasion of tolls by people going down Gaylins Lane.' The Trust had powers of supervision over the size of the wheels of vehicles using the Turnpike roads, and had a duty to stop and prevent nuisances on the roads, an example being the instruction to their Surveyor to give notice of prosecution to those people who permitted hogs to run loose on the roads and damage them.

The Trust allowed users of the Turnpikes to pay an annual fee to

5

permit them to travel on the highways without further payment,[17] and it is recorded that Joseph Doubleday, in the first year of the Trust's formation, 1769, compounded with the Trustees for liberty to pass through the Turnpikes of the Epping Trust without payment of further tolls for one year, for the payment of 10s. 6d. This figure was increased in 1790, a minute being passed which required all persons who wished to compound tolls on the Epping Turnpike road to pay double the amount previously paid.

Joseph, who appeared to be an active member of the Trust, was entrusted with a plan, in 1780, for reducing the gradient of Buckhurst Hill, as mentioned above, which contractors could inspect and for which work they could give their estimates, and on another occasion, in 1792, he became very concerned about the state of the road near the famous coaching inn, Epping Place, alleging that it was improperly sloped down at a spot which had been the scene of an accident in which a boy had been killed through the upsetting of a cart in which he had been riding, a number of other vehicles also meeting with accidents on this same piece of road. As a consequence, without waiting for the Trustees' consent, he made an outlay of 15 guineas for improvements to be put in hand, for which, however, they reimbursed him at a later date.

Benjamin Doubleday held the post of Treasurer to the Trust until he died in 1848, when his son Henry was appointed in his place; in 1833 the Treasurer's salary was fixed at £50 a year, the Surveyor's £25, and the Clerk to the Trust received £7 17s. 6d, so that it would appear that Benjamin's duties were far from negligible. The comparable figures for the Trust's earlier years are not available, but we know that in 1834 the salaries mentioned above were substantially increased, McAdam, the Surveyor, asking for 100 guineas, the Trust however offering £100, which was accepted. The Doubleday's connection with the Trust continued up to 1870, when the controlling power was transferred from local worthies to government officials in Whitehall.

The Minute Book of the Epping and Ongar Highway Trust contained, in 1817, an entry which read as follows:—'A forged £1 note was taken by the collector at one of the gates, but the Trustees made the loss good to the collector'. The note, which had been stamped FORGED in red and black ink in six places by the Bank of England was in all probability the one which was dated 1815, and had been endorsed by the signatures of Benjamin Doubleday and William

6

Hobbs; this note, described as obviously having seen much service, was in 1928 in the possession of the late C. B. Sworder of Epping.[18]

It is not clear when the Doubledays first appeared on the Essex scene,[19] but it seems probable that it was from the time of the rise of the Quakers in the middle of the 17th Century they became established there, and it is not possible to include within the scope of this sketch of Henry Doubleday and his times, their genealogical history through the centuries; nevertheless, perhaps some mention may be made of a few of his forebears of whom we have a little knowledge. Bridging the centuries from the time of the Domesday Book where the name is mentioned, and the night of the Gunpowder Plot, when a Captain Doubleday had a hand in the arrest of Guy Fawkes, we recall again Joseph Doubleday, Henry's grandfather, who took over the premises of the Inn at Epping displaying the sign of the Black Boy, in 1776. The Doubleday family appeared to be established in the area about this time for in the Essex Record Office are three Land Tax Assessments, dated 1782, for Joseph Doubleday of Waltham Holy Cross, a Mr. Doubleday[20] of Great Parndon, as well as Joseph Doubleday of Epping. When Joseph took over the Black Boy with its inn sign of great antiquity, trade signs were familiar sights hanging outside shop premises, and it is a matter of regret that they are no longer in use, although the Black Boy was until recently still used for hanging above tobacconists. A century ago seven inns[21] in the county of Essex sported this sign. It was in 1793 that Joseph Doubleday converted the Black Boy Inn into a grocer's shop; he is also described as a 'licensed alehouse keeper' and occupier of The White Horse in Epping in 1789, which was one of the total of seventeen inns[22] in that town. He died aged 76 on 16th May, 1838 and was laid to rest with others of his family in the Friends' Burial Ground beside the Meeting House at Epping.

There is clearly a connection between the Essex Doubledays and those living in Northumberland, for in the Essex Record Office there is a Deed dated 1762 in which 'Michael Doubleday of Alnwick Abbey in Northumberland, Esquire' is named as a party, and in about the year 1728 Thomas Story, the well known Quaker, recounted visiting a Friend, John Doubleday Jnr, near Alnwick, where he broke his journey whilst on his way from Carlisle to Edinburgh to attend the Quaker Yearly Meeting. He dined with John Doubleday, whose wife was the eldest daughter of Robert Barclay Senr. of Ury,[23] about 15 miles south of Aberdeen, and a daughter of 'the famous and honourable Robert Barclay, of the same place.'

An ancestor of Henry Doubleday, Francis Coleman, held some Essex land early in the 18th Century, which is described in the Abstract of Title deposited in the Essex Record Office as '5 acres of customary land formerly called Cooks lying within the Hamlett of Curley within the Manor of Woodham Walter . . . and those two parcels of meadow and also of certain lands called Bryans and Downes containing by estimation 18 acres.' From Francis Coleman this land passed to his descendants Robert and Elizabeth Doubleday and to their daughter Catherine Jane, and her brother-in-law William Paget, M.D. and his wife who was her sister, Mary Elizabeth. Attached to the Abstract is a very brief and imperfect pedigree of the Doubledays up to *circa* 1816. Among the numerous friends and correspondents of Henry Doubleday were members of the Paget family, in particular James (later Sir James) and Charles John ('C.J.') who were two brothers in a family of seventeen children whose father was Samuel Paget, the Yarmouth brewer. These two brothers were jointly responsible for bringing out the *Sketch of the Natural History of Great Yarmouth*' in 1834, and whilst the distinction as naturalists accorded to the Doubleday brothers was not theirs, it was rightly said that to a certain extent they did for Suffolk what our two Epping naturalists did for Essex. 'C.J.' and the two Doubleday brothers were founder members of the Entomological Club.

The Minutes of the Quaker Monthly Meeting which was held at Tottenham on 11th June 1835 contain a note that Henry's father Benjamin was appointed, together with Thomas Fowler, to attend to the repairs to the Meeting House roof at Epping, and it is known that this old thatched Meeting House, built in the middle of the 18th Century, lasted another ten years or so, Benjamin being chiefly responsible for its demolition and the erection of the present one in Hemnall Street Epping about the year 1845;[24] but little else of his life can be learned from Quaker records: at that time the tiny Epping Meeting was included within the area of Tottenham Monthly Meeting, but in 1871 the boundary of the neighbouring Monthly Meeting, Ratcliff and Barking, was extended to include a part of Essex, including Epping. A few members of the area so absorbed retained membership of Tottenham Monthly Meeting, but Henry's was transferred—he was, in fact, the only member of the Doubleday family then living in the Epping district. His parents had died many years before, as had his brother Edward, who in early life moved to Harrington Square in London, and whose 'Certificate of Removal' from Tottenham to Southwark Monthly Meeting was accepted, in accordance with Quaker practice, by Tottenham on '7th day of 7th month 1842'.[25]

Two years after Henry's death in 1875, his Coggeshall cousin William was moved to make a journey to visit Quaker families and meetings in the Quarterly Meeting area (London and Middlesex) which included Epping and other Meetings so well known to the Doubledays. He visited Tottenham on 'the 8th day of 2nd month 1877', where Tottenham Monthly Meeting was taking place 'in conjunction with women Friends', and a Minute records the event:— 'We have at this time the company of our Friend William Doubleday[26] of Coggeshall, from whom a Minute of Coggeshall Monthly Meeting, held at Bocking on the 4th day of 1st month last, has now been read, liberating him to visit the Meetings in our Quarterly Meeting and also to visit friends and their families as way may open.'

Another William Doubleday, who lived much earlier in the century, was also a prominent member of the Quakers; it fell upon him as Clerk[27] to the Coggeshall Monthly Meeting to sign the Minute 'disowning' Anna Buxton. This Meeting was held on the 5th day of 5th month 1806 at Halstead, and it was reported that her general deportment had over several years left a lot to be desired, and furthermore, she had now 'entered into an engagement for marriage with a person not of our society, which she is not at all disposed to relinquish . . .' Should the erring Anna change her ways, the Meeting said, membership would be restored! It is not clear whether she took advantage of the open door; fortunately, such narrow disciplinary rules of the Society are now things of the long distant past.

Possibly because of their plain dress and quaint speech the Quakers attracted some attention when gathering in large numbers for their meetings; in Coggeshall for instance, the day on which they met was known to the townspeople as the 'Quakers Washing-day',[28] as they fixed that day for the washing of blankets and other heavy articles, believing that Quakers brought fine weather with them; and in nearby Colchester Friends held a large annual gathering, afterwards taking part in a meal in which figured gooseberry-pie, and it was said that not until after this day were gooseberries to be bought

9

cheaply in the neighbourhood. As a consequence, Gooseberry Pie Day,[29] as the inhabitants called it, was eagerly awaited.

Henry Doubleday was meticulous and painstaking in all he did, not least in dealing expeditiously with matters which required his attention, and his prompt answering of letters from his numerous correspondents was spoken of with appreciation after his death. No doubt Epping Poor Law Union was gratified when he accepted the post of Treasurer upon his father's death in 1848; Henry was also an agent for that old established Fire Insurance Office, the 'Sun' which was formed in 1710 by Charles Povey at a time when only three other Fire Companies existed, viz: the Phoenix, the Friendly and the Hand-in-Hand, and he is shown as such in the Epping Post Office *Directory* of 1859. White's *Directory of Essex* of 1848, and also that of 1863, describe him as a grocer and Sun agent. The Post Office *Directory* for 1870 referred to him as a grocer and ironmonger, with no mention of the Sun, and that for 1874, the year preceding his death, he is merely noted as a resident.[30] As will be mentioned later, he lived the life of a recluse for the last few years, following a breakdown in health.

Although all his life he was of a quiet and retiring disposition, always serious minded and with little outward show of humour, yet certainly in his younger days he was an active and energetic townsman. In addition to his collections which were almost his life's work, his most valuable contribution to science was undoubtedly the compilation of the *Synonymic List of British Lepidoptera* which will be mentioned later. It is sad to record that most of the vast number of letters he wrote to fellow naturalists in this country and abroad have not survived; they undoubtedly contained much information which, whilst of considerable value to the recipient, was frequently not passed on for the benefit of other naturalists. Miller Christy, Henry Doubleday's young admirer, searched in vain after his death in 1875 for the diary which he was known to have kept and which was reputed to contain many observations on birds and insects.

In spite of his unassuming disposition, numerous friends testified to his genuinely warm welcome to visitors who called to see him, often with problems regarding identification of birds and insects, or to see his matchless collection of British and European lepidoptera. His extreme liberality[31] to fellow entomologists and to scientific bodies was widely recognised.

Had it not been for the ministration of a distant cousin, Ann Main, who devotedly looked after him and directed his household affairs for over thirty years, it is certain that Henry could not have carried on so long as he did, and our fund of knowledge would have been so much poorer. She was indeed, as his friend Dunning wrote after his death, to the Recluse of Epping as was Judith Bubb to the Man of Ross.[32]

And so we come to the last of the closely connected Epping and Coggeshall Doubledays, Thomas Puplett Doubleday,[33] who died in 1961; he was fond of recounting how his great grandfather Joseph Doubleday narrowly escaped attack by highwaymen[34] when on a journey to London to purchase goods. In the 18th century such journeys were not lightly undertaken, and as usual Joseph sent up prayers for a safe return, and to these he attributed his deliverance from the highwaymen, who on one occasion held up the stage coach before the one in which he was travelling and also the one following. Thomas was the nephew of Henry Doubleday[35] of Coggeshall, the seedsman who introduced Russian comfrey into Britain about the year 1870, as a fodder crop. Although undoubtedly a competent botanist Henry Doubleday of Coggeshall never achieved in his lifetime the outstanding recognition afforded to his cousin Henry of Epping as an entomologist. Thomas and his sister Edith, devoted members of the Society of Friends, were proud of their long Quaker ancestry and shortly before he died in 1961 the aged Thomas wrote of himself and all the Doubledays before him 'we realise the great Blessing to have known of God's care and love in our lives—The blessing of the Lord it maketh rich and He addeth no sorrow therewith.'

It is important that the two Quaker cousins, both named Henry Doubleday, should not be confused—one the seedsman and market-gardener of Coggeshall, whose pioneering work has been recognised by the adoption of his name by the Henry Doubleday Research Association, of Bocking, Essex, and the other, the subject of this memoir, the grocer-naturalist of Epping, whose reputation spread far beyond the confines of this island.

BIRDS IN DOUBLEDAY'S TIME

Henry Doubleday's particular enthusiasm as a naturalist in his earlier days was for ornithology, to which his contribution will be con-

11

sidered first, although it would be misleading to attempt a sharp division of his life into periods of special interests.

As with most forms of natural life, the birds in the Epping neighbourhood, and indeed the whole environs of London, were more varied and abundant in his time than today. It was recorded[36] that the Hawfinch, Wryneck, Red-backed Shrike, Grey Shrike, Nuthatch, Creeper, Nightingale, Missel-thrush, Flycatcher, Blackcap and Blue, Cole, Marsh, Ox-eye and Long-tailed Tits were familiar birds in the gardens of Lordship Lane, Tottenham, the area in which lived a number of Doubleday's Quaker friends, including, for a time the versatile Edward Newman. More than that, when the waters were out in the marshes there could be found 'wild geese (Grey and Brent), Ducks and Terns of various species, Snipes and Sand-pipers and other waders. One of the rarest visitors, the Cream-Coloured Courser was shot[37] in Hackney Marsh, just outside the Parish of Tottenham.' Up to the middle of the 19th century Great Bustards too frequented the heaths near Newmarket in Cambridgeshire, Royston in Hertfordshire and other suitable open country in the home counties, although they were possibly commoner on Salisbury Plain in Wiltshire than elsewhere in England. Doubleday, although adept at observing avian rarities, was apparently not fortunate enough to have spotted one of these huge but shy birds, although it was reported in the year 1871 that they were sighted in many counties from Somerset to Northumberland, and on many occasions it has been recorded from Essex.[38]

THE HEYSHAM LETTERS OF ORNITHOLOGICAL INTEREST

Edward Doubleday, when he was twenty years old, visited the well-known naturalist Dr. T. C. Heysham of Carlisle in 1831: the reason for the meeting is not clear, but Edward suggested to Heysham that he should correspond with his brother Henry, at home in Epping, and exchange notes and views on subjects of mutual interest, chiefly ornithology. So started a correspondence which lasted at least for fifteen years;[39] the letters to Heysham became the property of Mr. J. G. Mounsey, and Miller Christy,[40] when compiling his book *Birds of Essex* (1890) was fortunate enough to have had the opportunity of studying them at leisure, and drawing upon the information contained in them. The one-hundred-and-one letters to which Christy had access threw considerable light on Doubleday's private opinions and on the passing events of his life, but only the brief extracts quoted by Miller Christy are known to us; these were frequently the results of Henry's own careful observations, of which Miller Christy made full use in *Birds of Essex*, which for many years was the standard source of reference on the birds of Doubleday's native county.

The importance of carefully dating and indicating the localities whence rare birds were obtained or observed was not always appreciated by Doubleday in his early years, and this is rightly deplored by Miller Christy, although as he pointed out many years later, in 1887, 'the best Ornithologists up to a few years ago took no account of localities'; it was indeed a failing not confined by any means to ornithologists.

In the first letter, an extract from which appears below, it is interesting to observe the Quaker phraseology, although Miller Christy tells us that Henry, in his later letters, used 'you' in place of the plain 'thee' or 'thou'. A list of 153 birds which Doubleday had collected was attached to the letter.

Epping, 8th Mo. 30th 1831.

'In the first place I must return thee my sincere thanks for the polite attention paid to my brother during his short stop at Carlisle, and also for thy kind offer to assist me in my ornithological pursuits.

For the past three years I have devoted nearly all my leisure time to ornithology and entomology, and considering that my time is often closely occupied with other affairs, I have made considerable progress, particularly in birds, as thee will see by the annexed list of those I possess, nearly all of which I have preserved myself. I have added the arrival of the summer birds at Epping, as I thought it would be interesting to thee to compare it with their arrival in your neighbourhood, as you have most of them in the north. In the account of them (i.e. *the summer birds of passage at Carlisle*) published in the *Philosophical Magazine* (Vol. VIII 1830, p. 444) (which has greatly pleased me) I do not see the Chiff Chaff mentioned. Do you not have it? It is very common here . . . I find more difficulty in procuring the Hawks than anything else, as the forest-keepers have almost exterminated them here,[41] and we see nothing but a solitary Kestrel and Sparrow-Hawk, and even these but rarely . . . The *Water Ouzel, Dotterel*, and, indeed, any others not in the list, I should be very glad of;

13

and as I have been thus free in stating my wants, I hope thee will be equally free in stating thine, as nothing would give me greater pleasure than in supplying thee with either birds or insects. At present I do not know what to offer, but if a male Garganey would be of any use to thee, it is quite at thy service. I procured and stuffed it about three months since and it is in very fine plumage.

I have succeeded well in my attempts to keep the summer warblers alive in confinement and have now four beautiful male Nightingales, three Blackcaps, two Greater Pettychaps,[42] Common Whitethroat, and one Lesser Whitethroat. They have now just done moulting and are coming into song. They are in beautiful plumage and in the most perfect health, and will sing all through the winter if kept sufficiently warm . . .

I do not think Selby's arrangements of the birds good; nor do I think he has genera enough. In many instances I prefer the genera as given in Dr. Fleming's work, though some of his are not natural. Genera, to be good, ought to be distinguishable at first sight, and artificial ones are good for nothing . . . I am a strong advocate for the foundation of genera, founded on the consideration of every habit and character, instead of having a heterogeneous mass lumped together with a generic name.

The change of plumage in birds is another subject in which I feel a great interest . . .'

It was stated the rather irregular, but quite legible handwriting was a fair sample of the letters of Henry Doubleday, who was then in his early twenties; as he grew older his more mature handwriting developed which, even in his later years after experiencing long periods of mental disturbance, drew comments of appreciation for its clarity and style; and no doubt he had to pay particular attention to these when carrying on his correspondence, which was voluminous, with his European colleagues.

Although Doubleday realised that there was no substitute for careful observation of birds in their wild surroundings, he kept a number of birds alive, sometimes over long periods, during which he could study their habits at leisure; when he wrote to Heysham in November 1831 he mentioned that he had paid considerable attention to the nest and eggs of birds, having in his collection most of the eggs of those birds which lived in the Epping neighbourhood. In spite of the thinning out of the warblers and nightingales by London birdcatchers, the miles of Forest still ensured that these birds and the various species of Willow Wren, Whitethroat, Blackcaps and Pettychaps continued to flourish there. It is true to say that Doubleday was no mere collector of birds, although at that time ornithologists relied on the gun to add specimens to their collections, and Doubleday was certainly no exception; in fact his prowess with a gun was well recognised. But photography, which in later life fascinated him,[43] was unfortunately not sufficiently developed in his earlier years to enable him to substitute the camera for his gun. During his life-time naturalists became concerned at the threat to wild life by the indiscriminate shooting of rare birds, usually, it must be said, by ignorant country people having no real interest in birds, who let fly with a gun at any strange bird unfortunate enough to venture within its range. We have no record of Doubleday acquiring specimens by other methods commonly used, such as knocking them down with poles after being found in an exhausted state, or catching them with a dog; such cruelty is not unknown in our times, as this extract from a Saffron Walden paper[44] in 1963, illustrates:—

'One local railway worker managed to stalk a lone goose one morning last week and so tired was the bird that the man was able to get close enough to hit it over the head with an elder stick. However, the stick broke and the bird, believed to be a pink-footed goose, escaped.' Instances such as this are occasionally to be found in Christy's *Birds of Essex*, but we cannot put too much blame on, for example, a farm worker who obtained a goose in this way bearing in mind the hard existence for such people a hundred years ago.

In January 1832 Doubleday referred to his nightingales and blackcaps singing all day, and the occasional song of the pettychaps, and four years later, on February 13th 1836 he wrote once more 'my nightingales are singing delightfully'. Many were the birds he kept in captivity for observation, one being the Redwing about which he wrote in 1831:—

'I have now alive a Redwing I got last January' (he wrote this in November), 'and in August it moulted; but instead of the usual colours it has become a perfect black'. He contributed a long letter[45] giving information on the food and song of this bird to the *Zoologist* in 1864. The *Zoologist* also received a letter from him in 1843 in which he described the habits of a Great Gray Shrike which he kept alive in a cage for a long time; this bird which was acquired from a local bird-catcher, is extremely rare in the Epping Forest district; he related how the bird invariably hung up its food in the cage: if

15

half-a-dozen small birds were put in, the Shrike would hang them all up by forcing their heads through the wires of the cage, and pieces of meat were hung up in a similar way. Needless to say the birds were dead when put into the cage. The other bird of this genus, the Red-backed Shrike or Butcher Bird, although common as a summer visitor to the Forest, appeared, it was said, to be decreasing in numbers.

One of the birds upon which Doubleday made some particularly valuable observations was the Hawfinch, Yarrell's account of it in his *History of British Birds*[46] consisting very largely of contributions from him. He drew extensively on his friend's unique knowledge of the habits of that bird. The *Dictionary of National Biography* quotes Doubleday's note on the Hawfinch in the *Magazine of Zoology*[47] in 1837 as being probably his first contribution to science, but his first reference to this bird appears to be in a letter to Heysham dated June 12th 1832: an extract of this letter, quoted by Miller Christy, reads as follows:—

'I am happy in being able to send one rarity, viz:—two eggs of the Hawfinch which till this spring I never saw. The nest is built in the most careless manner and consists of a few coarse sticks, then a layer of that coarse lichen which grows on the stems of oaks and (is) lined with a few roots. It is also extremely shallow. They seem to build in any situation. The nest I took was in a whitethorn, about four feet high, and I saw one on the top of a tall spruce fir . . . I have now a full grown young Hawfinch in confinement which was caught in our forest about a fortnight ago.' A few years later he was rearing Hawfinches, as he disclosed in a letter to Heysham in 1836—'I have brought up some young ones this summer, and have just sent three to our friend Thomas Allis' (of York), and again to Heysham a month later, 'I have no doubt I can get some more Hawfinches for thee. Mine is still alive and well. The nest is so loose that it can hardly be moved without falling to pieces—in fact it is the clumsiest nest I am acquainted with. It has been found in Kent, but rarely, as Mr. Yarrell had not a British specimen of its egg until I gave him one about a month ago.'[48]

Henry Doubleday kept records for eighteen consecutive years of twenty-five of our common summer migrants and his thoroughness in compiling these led Miller Christy to comment that they were probably the most complete of their kind ever gathered by one man by his own observation, and indeed it was no mean feat for one

16

Epping 3rd day evening

My dear Uncle,

Aunt Clemence Smith has brought me thy letter that I may reply to it — My dear father is not sufficiently conscious to say whether he would like to see thee if asked the question — he has, I believe, not made the slightest inquiry about any one — indeed he says very little — and I consider all hangs on a thread which may be snapped any moment but it is possible he may survive some little time — also he is evidently much weaker — Ann Main called me up this morning about 2 o'clock and thought him much worse but after a fit of sickness went to sleep again. If thee wishes to come over directly I think father would know thee, provided no sudden change takes place, but he is quite incapable of conversation — Excuse this hurried note and assuring thee I should be glad to see thee

believe me with our united dear love

Thy aff. nephew HD

A specimen of Henry Doubleday's handwriting

The plaque on the site of Henry Doubleday's shop

busily engaged in other matters. These records, which were extracted by Miller Christy from the Heysham letters and the *Zoologist*, were published by him in his *History of the Birds of Essex* in the *Table of observations on the arrival of the summer migrants at Epping* (1828–1845).[49] The Rev. Revett Sheppard kept similar records at Wrabness in Essex for the years 1818–1830, which were mostly published in *Transactions of the Linnean Society*, but some were also included in letters to Heysham from Sheppard's son. Sheppard's records were also published in *Birds of Essex*.[50]

For his book Miller Christy naturally drew on many sources besides the Heysham letters for his information, in particular three bird lists were mentioned which were of special value in the compilation of what was the first chronicle of Essex birds. They were Henry's brother Edward's *Catalogue of Birds which have occurred in the neighbourhood of Epping*, William Doubleday King's[51] *List of Birds found in the neighbourhood of Sudbury*, and lastly, George Day's articles on the *Birds of Essex*. One hundred and twenty-five species were included in Edward Doubleday's list, which was published in 1835 in Volume 3 of the *Entomological Magazine*, one hundred and thirty in the compilation of W. D. King, Henry's first cousin, which was printed in 1838 in Fulcher's *Sudbury Magazine*; and lastly, the *Chelmsford Chronicle* in 1880 carried Day's seven articles on Essex birds,[52] but which contained little original matter. In introducing his list Edward Doubleday paid generous tribute to his brother, confirming his great interest in ornithology at that time: 'I have first to state, that I owe all my knowledge of Ornithology, or nearly all, to my brother. With his beautiful collection of British birds always before my eye, continually hearing his remarks on them and their habits, I have gained knowledge without labour, without study.'

After rejection of a score or more reputed visitors to Essex, owing to insufficient evidence or circumstances making their identity doubtful, Miller Christy was still able to list 272 species, and when he died in 1928 his unpublished supplement was of considerable assistance to Glegg when gathering material for his more up to date work, *History of the Birds of Essex*, published the following year.

From time to time Doubleday added to the British Museum's collection of birds, many different species being presented over the years, including the Gray (*sic*) Plover, Curlew—Sandpiper, Little Stint, and a pair of Rough-legged Buzzards, which were killed at

Epping; many different birds were attracted to the numerous ponds in Epping Forest, and these were by no means neglected by Doubleday, who recorded many captures on their banks, including two Green Sandpipers which he shot and gave to the British Museum.[53] It was of this bird he wrote in 1832,[54] 'I have met with no ornithological rarities except . . . a very fine specimen of the Green Sandpiper which I shot here about two weeks since without spoiling a feather, and it has made a very nice bird. It is very rare here and only now and then met with in the months of July, August and September. I cannot view it in the light of a Winter visitant as I never heard or saw one at that season . . . I should think it is a Summer visitor like the Common Sandpiper,[55] though a much rarer one.' In later years he met with it more frequently, in one year, 1840, as late as 2nd November: on that occasion he shot at, but only slightly wounded the Green Sandpiper which he kept in his room, where we are told, it soon became very tame, moving rapidly about and feeding readily upon small worms.[56] At this time both Henry's parents were alive, and one wonders how far his enthusiasm for ornithology was shared by them. It was this bird which Miller Christy described as most mysterious—its eggs had never been taken in Britain, yet a record had been made almost every month of its occurrence in Essex alone.

It was not only the Forest ponds which attracted Doubleday but water in the inland creeks of the Essex coastline and the isolated saltings and marshes lured him from the shop-counter to study the many waders and sea-birds to be found there. These journeys were usually made in the company of friends or relatives with similar interests, many additions to his collection being made on these excursions. Walton-on-the-Naze appeared to be a favourite haunt, and it was there in 1833 that he shot several Curlew-Sandpipers, and it was probably one of these which he presented to the British Museum in 1833.[57]

HIS SKILL IN TAXIDERMY

As mentioned earlier, many birds were given to the British Museum, as well as to the Saffron Walden Museum, but in spite of this he recorded in 1833 that he possessed 216 skins of British birds, when he was 24 years old; by this time he had become a first-class shot

and an outstanding taxidermist, his high degree of skill in stuffing and mounting birds receiving recognition from Heysham, to whose letter he replied with characteristic modesty on 31st August 1834:—
'I am sure you praise my efforts at setting up birds far too highly . . . I have done the best I could, but it often happens that business interrupts me when I am about a bird and I have to leave it for an hour or two . . . You must recollect that I am perfectly self-taught.'

Many years later at the Great Exhibition of 1851 his work earned extravagant praise from Edward Newman in the *Zoologist*,[58] in which he mentioned that of all the countries contributing examples of taxidermy to this Exhibition, Würtemburg stood unrivalled, but he continued:—'In this country the art of bird-stuffing has, in a limited number of hands, attained great excellence, and the modest aim of our greatest artists has been to represent repose: in this no-one has surpassed Henry Doubleday; there is a great truthfulness in his birds that defies criticism; it consists not in mere smoothness of feather, but in a faithful version of the figure: he preserves the exact contour; like Bewick he is a student of Nature, and so has transferred to the inanimate skin, as Bewick to the inanimate wood, all the attributes of life that can exist without absolute vitality: and moreover, he never fails to place a bird on the centre of gravity, a trait, in which he stands almost alone.'

SEA-BIRDS

Walton-on-the-Naze was also the destination of a winter visit by Doubleday in company with his relative Jonathan Grubb, where in one December he obtained specimens of the Common Tern, which was reported in the *Zoologist*. Edward Doubleday also recorded that a specimen of this bird was killed at Epping in 1835, obviously driven inland by rough weather; a few Essex records have also been made of another sea-bird, Leach's Fork-tailed Petrel, which had been carried a considerable distance from the coast; on 20th January 1837 a fine specimen was found by a boy in Epping Forest and taken to Doubleday, and another was picked up dead in a field near Epping, about the middle of November 1840, on each occasion following a storm. Both birds were retained in his collection, until dispersed in his sale in 1871.[59]

THE BLUE-HEADED YELLOW WAGTAIL, AND THE LITTLE RINGED PLOVER

Perhaps Doubleday's most exciting ornithological experience at Walton or indeed elsewhere was the recording in 1834 of the Blue-headed Yellow Wagtail for the first time in Great Britain.[60] This continental bird, a rare visitor to these islands, was described in a letter to Heysham as follows:

'On the 3rd October, walking with two friends on the top of the cliffs at *Walton-on-the-Naze*, I had the pleasure of seeing two individuals of the Gray Headed Yellow Wagtail (*Motacilla neglecta* of Gould), one of which (a male) I fortunately shot, thus proving that this bird occasionally at least, visits this country. Although, being in its autumnal plumage, the marks are not so well defined as in spring, yet there can be no doubt of the species. The whole underparts are pure yellow, except the chin; this and the eye-streak are pure white. The head and back of the neck are light bluish-grey, tinged with brown at the tips of the feathers . . . the back clear olive-green. When I came to London I took it to Bruton Street (where the Museum of the Zoological Society then was) and there I met with Bennett, Gould and Yarrell, all of whom at once pronounced it *Neglecta*.'

Miller Christy also recorded that Doubleday was the first person to observe the Little Ringed Plover in this country, which he did in 1845 at Shoreham, where he obtained a specimen, although at the date of publication of Miller Christy's book (1890) no record of its appearance in Essex had been made.

THE NOMENCLATURE OF BIRDS

So interested was Doubleday in his study of birds, and throughout his life this was never extinguished, that he decided to bring out a revised catalogue of all the species occurring in Great Britain and Ireland. Whilst this effort systematically to catalogue the species, which he based mainly on the genera and species of Jenyns' *Manual of British Invertebrated Animals*, was undoubtedly a step forward in British ornithology, it was reviewed rather severely, and cannot be considered of great importance. The publication, which was entitled *A Nomenclature of British Birds*,[61] was brought out in 1836, and ran through several editions, the last being the fourth, in 1845. The

Rev. F. O. Morris in his well-known *History of British Birds* (1847) was among those who had doubts of this list, writing:—

'I must here express my opinion that far too great a number of new genera have been introduced by modern naturalists: take, for example, Mr. Doubleday's otherwise excellent catalogue of British Birds. In this we find eleven species of owl, given every one of them with a different generic name . . .'

He is critical also of the classification of other birds, including the four species of swallows and martins, which Doubleday put into four genera. Of his objections Morris says, 'A fault indeed not of the individual author of it, but of the whole modern system—his only, so far as he has fallen in and coincided with it.'

HIS ASSISTANCE TO YARRELL

Yarrell was particularly indebted to Doubleday for a great deal of the information regarding the plumage of birds, and of their nesting habits and eggs, which he incorporated in his book, and they apparently worked closely together in gathering information and settling problems. 'During a visit I have recently been paying to my friend Wm. Yarrell,' wrote Doubleday to Heysham on 24th January 1837, 'we had a thorough look through the London collections of birds and insects. There are a few points respecting some of our British Birds that we are very anxious to clear up, especially as Mr. Yarrell is about to commence a work on British Birds to correspond with his Fishes.'[62]

The correspondence between Yarrell and Doubleday spanned many years, numbers of birds being given or lent to Yarrell for description and illustration; the rare American Scaup for example, which figured in a woodcut in *British Birds* was obtained by Doubleday 'in the London market.'[63] and Yarrell related that Henry Doubleday had favoured him with the loan of a young Two-barred Crossbill, which he had shot himself in his own garden at Epping,[64] and this is recorded in the later editions of Yarrell's book: in fact three specimens of this extremely rare bird, including the young one mentioned above, were lent by Doubleday to Yarrell. Professor Newton, who, with Howard Saunders edited the 4th edition of Yarrell's book (1871–1885), said: 'Somewhere about the same time (1846), it is believed Doubleday shot a young bird in his own garden at Epping.' Newton's doubt seems quite groundless, as Doubleday was familiar with the two other Crossbills, the Common and the Parrot Crossbill, and specifically mentioned having also shot the Common Crossbill at Epping, in the same letter to the *Zoologist* in which he recorded the Two-barred Crossbill. The bird was kept by Doubleday until his cases of birds were sold in 1871, and this specimen, together with seven Common Crossbills were purchased for thirty-six shillings. The first Common Crossbill was seen by Doubleday at Epping on March 9th 1833, and he lent about a dozen specimens to Yarrell for illustration. The two adult Two-barred Crossbills which Doubleday lent to Yarrell were given by Doubleday to his friend Richard Dix,[65] and upon Dix's early death in 1872 these two birds, described as the rarest in his collection, passed by his special request, to Henry Stevenson of Norwich, who described them as European White-winged Crossbills (*Loxia bifasciata*): to avoid confusion Edward Newman referred to it as the European or Two-barred Crossbill, as he was advised that Salmon had added the White-winged Crossbill to the *List of Godalming birds*, which as Doubleday pointed out to Newman, could be mistaken for the American White-winged Crossbill, quite a different bird. *Loxia leucoptera*, the White-winged Crossbill was thenceforth generally adopted for the Crossbill of the New World.

The Parrot Crossbill, which is a very rare visitor to these islands, is the North European form of the Common Crossbill: when writing[66] of an incident in 1861 in which no less than three specimens were killed in one shot by a boy at Lambourne in Essex, Doubleday commented, 'This is the first occurrence of this species in this neighbourhood so far as I am aware," but he apparently overlooked Yarrell's reference to one which was obtained by Mr. Blyth in the autumn of 1835 in Epping Forest.

Numerous communications from Doubleday to scientific magazines, authors of books on ornithology and to friends and fellow naturalists contained a great deal of first-hand information, and make interesting reading, but it would be tedious to catalogue them all, and would be outside the scope of this brief sketch of his life and work. There must be very few birds in the British list to which he did not add at one time some fresh details of habits or plumage, and indeed the latter aspect of ornithology received particular attention throughout his life: in spite of his increasing involvement with the study and classification of lepidoptera in later years, his interest in birds never waned; in the month before his death he contributed to the *Zoologist*[67] a long and valuable criticism of John Hancock's work *A Catalogue of the Birds of Northumberland and Durham*: Doubleday's notice of the *Catalogue* extended over eight pages, and included many instances of his own observations of bird-life, referring particularly to the adult plumage of birds of prey, to the Hooded Crow, Crossbill, Linnet, Redpoll, Wagtail, Grouse and others. Some examples of his interesting comments on these and other birds are given in the Appendix.[68]

THE PARIS JOURNEY

Lacking perhaps the adventurous spirit of his brother, or because of compelling restrictions, Henry Doubleday apparently left his native land but once,[69] and his concern must have been strong for him to have taken that step. The reason for his visit to a foreign country was to enable him to meet French lepidopterists and to study Parisian collections of which he had heard and read so much. In comparing English specimens of butterflies and moths with Continental ones he hoped to be able to avoid in future the confusion then obtaining which resulted from differences in nomenclature. Clearly, a reliable internationally acceptable catalogue to obviate duplication of names would be of immense value, and it was his aim to provide this. As a result, the most important work of his life was undertaken: it was the preparation of the *Synonymic List of British Lepidoptera*, commenced soon after his return from Paris. Published in instalments at intervals between 1847 and 1850, it made a considerable impact, and its importance to science was immediately recognised. A great deal of time was taken up in Doubleday's later years by its revision.

It was in July 1843 that the Paris journey was made—a vastly different undertaking from a similar trip today—and we may wonder how this modest tradesman from the quiet country town of Epping fared in the bustle of the French capital. No doubt his brother Edward and probably his entomological companion James English assisted in the management of the shop during Henry's absence. Although very few records of the trip exist, we know that while in Paris he took every available opportunity of meeting fellow natura-lists and examining their collections,[70] comparing the names of English moths, particularly the *Noctuae* and *Bombyces*, with their specimens, finding time also to enjoy some collecting in the environs of Paris. This historic visit would have achieved a more intimate and colourful interest had the diary which Doubleday kept been found; we know no details of the trip or even where in Paris he stayed, although it would be surprising had he not been the guest of his correspondent Achille Guenée at Châteaudun;[71] with his simple tastes and modest bearing he would indeed have been a welcome visitor, having so few requirements. For the more personal details of the visit we must therefore draw upon our imagination, although his burning enthusiasm for natural history doubtless left little time for other interests, especially as his absence from home amounted to no more than twelve days—he left on 21st July and returned to his home in Epping on the evening of 2nd August 1843. Had he not been Guenée's guest, he would have been able to stay in Paris and be looked after reasonably well for a modest sum—a contemporary essayist noting that he could, for example, have taken a single well-furnished room at the Hotel des Etrangers in the Rue Vivienne for 3 frs. a day and paid 2 frs. for a good dinner. A necessary addition would have been a wax candle, one of which would have lasted for the duration of his stay, and a fire in his room would have been extra, but hardly necessary in July. '10 sous a day would have satisfied the servants, and in contrast to the cheaper eating-houses in London, a clean napkin would have been laid at meals, and all little comforts would have been provided.'[72]

The name of Achille Guenée has been mentioned, and it is clear that for Henry Doubleday this lawyer from Châteaudun stood out head and shoulders above his fellow European lepidopterists, as indeed Doubleday himself was often regarded among British entomologists by his fellows. The ties of friendship between the two men were greatly strengthened by the Paris visit, and few opportunities were lost by either naturalist in acknowledging his debt to the other. Guenée, for example, in the Introduction to his work *Uranides et Phalenites* paid generous tribute to the man with whom he had co-operated in research over many years. After thanking those entomologists who had assisted him, he wrote:—

'Lastly, I cannot resist the pleasure of closing this list by a name that I know not how to repeat too often, that of my excellent and useful friend, Henry Doubleday of Epping, who seems to have devoted to my work and even to the enriching of my collection, a more active zeal than that used by many others in their own interests.'

It is likely that Guenée paid a return visit to Doubleday at his home at Epping some 10 years later, for Richard Weaver of Birmingham, writing in the *Zoologist*, mentioned that in 1854 he sent some larvae of *Lasiocampa callunae*,[73] the Scottish Eggar, to Doubleday with whom an eminent French naturalist was then staying. This visitor was probably his friend Achille Guenée.

THE GAZE LETTERS

It was not long after his return home that Henry Doubleday intimated in a letter dated March 1844 to his friend William H. Gaze[74] his intention of cataloguing the English lepidoptera. Gaze, who was a Customs and Excise official living at Ballingdon near Sudbury in Suffolk exchanged many insects with Doubleday, who frequently met him when visiting relatives at Sudbury.

The letter read as follows:—

'Epping, 6th March 1844.

My dear Sir,

I have taken the earliest opportunity since my return to look out a few Lepidoptera for you and only wish they were better, but if I live I have no doubt I can do much more for you. I have only one (*f.*) *Hyale* left and that is not well set—it is not my own taking—the (*m.*) one caught here—I have also sent the three best specimens I have left of *Edusa*—I think they are finer than those you possess—I have put in a specimen of the true *Pyrausta cespitalis*, you will see it is totally different from *Phytometra aenea*. I am very desirous of making up my sets of the Lepidoptera with a view to a correct catalogue of all the British species—there are a few you possess which if you do not mind parting I should be very glad of one—you have two males of *Cleora cinctaria*. I have not a male but two females and have sent one thinking you might have no objection to give a male for a female then we shall have each a pair. I also should be very glad of one *berberata*—one of that dusky *Geometra* allied to or a variety of *E. impluviata*; and if you would part with the larger specimen of *Geometra fuscantaria*— I strongly suspect this is a mere variety of *erosaria* . . . I shall always be most happy to send anything in my power to add to

25

your collection and have no doubt if nothing unforeseen occurs to prevent me I shall be able to send you many things.

Insects are fast coming out—I have seen several of the early moths—if you have a chance you would get many things as soon as the sallows are in flower if you beat them at night into a net. There is an *Orthosia* allied to *mistabilis* with more pectinnated antennae in the male—it is *populeti* of Fabricius[75] and *subplumbea* of Haworth—I much want a good series of this—I have several but not fine—I think Sudbury a likely locality for it—I should much like to see your captures of anything you do not know as you take them. I would return the specimens free of expense and say if they were worth looking after.

I sincerely hope that some of the things I send may be acceptable and with my kindest regards and assuring you I shall ever be willing to serve you in any way in my power, believe me,
My dear Sir,
Every Yours most sincerely,
Henry Doubleday.

I put in a few pins of the size I use for moths—of course the *Tineae* want finer—these I can send you at any time if you wish. To Mr. Wm. H. Gaze, Ballingdon.'

Attached to this letter was a separate sheet containing a list of 56 different species of lepidoptera, which Doubleday enclosed for Gaze. Many of these were male and female of the same species and also a number of varieties were included.

The year 1843 was not a good year for *Colias hyale* (Pale Clouded Yellow) in the Epping district where only about a dozen specimens were captured in August and September. No doubt William Gaze would have been more fortunate had Doubleday written to him the previous year, when these butterflies were more numerous in Epping.[76]

A further letter was written on 15th March 1844, in which Doubleday acknowledged some insects from Gaze:—

'Epping. March 15th 1844.
My dear Sir,
Many thanks for the insects you so kindly sent—I am truly obliged to you for them. The moth which seems a variety of *E. impluviata* is much larger than those found near London.

Mr. Bentley must have accidentally made a mistake in the name and I think you are also mistaken in the application of the name "*Hovudaria*": this name was applied by Haworth to a small and very dark variety of *elutata* (the July Moth) found in Cumberland. It is very probably a distinct species—I do not think it has ever been applied to a variety of *impluviata*.

I have little doubt I can procure you *Thecla pruni*[77] this season. I will send a person to Monk's Wood to look after them as I want to get a lot if I can—I wish you could send me a catalogue of what you have marking all those where you would like better specimens—I shall be truly glad to assist you by any means in my power. There is no way of getting a collection without Entomologists will mutually assist each other and I shall always be glad to send anything which I can procure. I quite believe a vast many good things are to be taken at Sudbury. *Cidaria quadrifasciaria* of Stephens I know abounds and I should be glad of 2 or 3 dozens of this kind. Also *C. sylvaticata* which I think is also common—*Eupithecia venosata* and other species of this genus I know occur. The best way is to get all you can of anything which you do not know to be universally common. I have no doubt you would do much by means of sugar—but it wants perseverance and it is much better to keep to one likely spot than to roam about.
The weather is now very bad for the early moths and but very little is to be done at present. I hope it may soon change—I keep breeding a few things such as *Orthosia* etc.

Mr. Dale spent yesterday with me here. He has not been in London for some time before—he is much struck with the alterations at the British Museum.

As it is nearly post time you must excuse more at this time and with my best wishes and many thanks, believe me, my dear Sir,

Yours very sincerely,
Henry Doubleday.'

The *Thecla pruni* (Black Hairstreak) which Doubleday promised Gaze were referred to again in a letter dated some 9 months later, sent with a package of 16 specimens, including 4 *pruni*: but the list unfortunately omitted any data. The exchange of insects which Doubleday carried out with numerous correspondents in Britain and

27

the Continent was clearly to their mutual advantage, which the letter shows:—

'Epping. January 1st 1845.

My dear Sir,

I have looked out what specimens I can that you are likely to want and among these are some rare species. I was much disappointed about *Thecla pruni*. I only received a dozen—all bad—I send you the best four of the lot.

If you do not think the insects sent an equivalent for your *Eupithecia* I will return it to you immediately upon hearing from you. In great haste, believe me, with best wishes, Dear Sir,

Yours most truly,

Henry Doubleday.'

The last of the Gaze letters to which reference is made at this point is dated 20th November 1845, and is reproduced below. On this occasion Doubleday enclosed 20 specimens, including in the list the scientific name and the town of capture—except that for some insects only a vague location such as 'Scotland' is given, but again omitting dates with the exception of one, and then only 'Scotland, Summer 1845'.

'Epping. November 20th 1845.

To William Gaze.

My dear Sir,

I have now put a few insects into a box for you and only wish I had more to send worth your having, but I really have nothing else that I think would be of any use to you—I hope some of these now sent may be useful—you will see how very different the Scotch *vetusta* is from the Epping one—all I have seen from Scotland are the same. Don't you ever mean to come this way? I should be very glad to show you my collection—please to write and say if you get them safe and with best wishes believe me, My dear Sir,

Yours most sincerely,

Henry Doubleday.'

THE SYNONYMIC LIST OF BRITISH LEPIDOPTERA

To return now to Doubleday's *Catalogue* it would not be an exaggeration to say, with Miller Christy, that its completion almost marked the end of an epoch in British entomology. Newman, predictably, was full of praise devoting a full page of the *Zoologist* to a review, and reproducing a page from it to illustrate Doubleday's plan of nomenclature. The generic and specific names were given by Doubleday and these were decided by clearing away a mass of errors, proved by actual examination and comparison with authentic specimens, of which many thousands must have passed through his hands. To quote Newman, 'It frequently happens that when a work has long been talked of, it disappoints us at last: in the present instance, the reverse is the case: nothing can be more carefully compiled than the list before us, nothing more completely adapted to the purpose for which it is intended.'[78]

The first instalment of the first edition of the *Catalogue* was published in October 1847 and the last part in December 1849,[79] the whole taking the form of a list of British butterflies and moths, excluding the *Tineina*. It was 10 years later that the second and more complete edition appeared, which included all the microlepidoptera, and further supplements were issued in 1866 and lastly in 1873. The final catalogue brought the number of recognised British species of lepidoptera to nearly 2,100.

Doubleday was reluctant, as always, to be drawn into arguments in defence of his *List*, but he was always quick to acknowledge fair criticism, apparently caring little for any personal credit, but only for the advancement of the science upon which he had set his heart. When but a young man of some twenty-three summers he wrote[80] to his friend Heysham, with whom he had only recently formed a friendship which was to last many years:—'Every person has clearly a right to his own opinions, and I think that nothing does more injury to science than one person assuming a kind of dictatorship and expecting everybody to bow to his decision.'

When Newman published his book on Moths in 1869, after describing the *Nolidae*,[81] before going on with his description of the Footman and Muslin Moths (the *Lithosiidae*) he drew the attention of his readers, especially the junior ones, to Doubleday's *List*, and again he was unstinting in his praise of the man and his work. He commented as follows:—'The little family of *Nolidae* we should have included with the larger family which here follows and is called *Lithosiidae*, but Mr. Doubleday, in the work mentioned below, has separated them and no one is so well acquainted with the subject. At this point of our *History of British Moths* we should like to make an observation on the English names. We consider these names are often very silly and unmeaning, but still we use them because we do not wish our juvenile readers to be deterred from the study of

29

Entomology, which is a truly delightful study, by long Latin words very often without any meaning and sometimes also difficult to pronounce; still, as these names must be learned by and by, we always add them at the end of each description. These names we obtain from a printed catalogue, called *A List of British Butterflies and Moths* by Henry Doubleday. This is the most perfect and complete scientific work ever published in this country and, although it cost 2s., we recommend every one of our young entomological friends to buy it, because it will enable them to obtain a thorough knowledge of the mode of arranging these beautiful objects. The list can be bought of every bookseller and naturalist in the Kingdom and one copy will last a lifetime. Mr. Henry Doubleday, the author, lives at Epping and knows more of British Butterflies and Moths than all the other Entomologists in the Kingdom, he never sells nor deals in books nor insects, but has acquired all his knowledge solely to gratify his ardent love of the science, and for the purpose of instructing others—an example we cannot too highly recommend to our entomological friends.'

This is praise indeed, but it should be remembered that of all the people who helped Newman in this work, Doubleday's contribution was by far the greatest, inevitably putting the author under a debt of gratitude to him. Nevertheless, it is clear that the admiration which Newman had for his fellow Quaker lasted throughout his life. In the preface of the book mentioned above Newman acknowledged his great obligation to Doubleday, and at the same time excused his own shortcomings by emphasizing the catholicism of his own entomological studies. This is how he put it:—

'An imperative but most agreeable duty remains—that of thanking those kind friends who have rendered me such important services during the progress of this work. And first Mr. Doubleday, through whose hands every sheet and every column has passed. Many omissions have been supplied and many errors expunged An almost perfect blank has hitherto existed as to the times of appearance of our lepidoptera in the perfect state and my own experience was insufficient to supply this blank.

Although for many years I was an assiduous collector of insects, I never gave that especial attention to lepidoptera which they have received at the hands of my friend. The collections of *Diptera*, *Hymenoptera*, *Coleoptera* and *Neuroptera* under my care, attest the fact that my attention has been equally divided amongst all classes of insects, and it is next to impossible to acquire anything approaching a perfect knowledge of the times of appearance of every species. Mr. Doubleday has abundantly made up for my shortcomings in this respect and has supplied me with information which, in many instances, has never before appeared in print. Then again the *Eupitheciae* and the *Leucanidae* have undergone a revision at his hands; he has found it necessary to alter a few names, generic as well as specific and to institute a few new combinations.'

In 1870 Newman published in the *Entomologist* a long article,[82] running to 10 pages, on the classification of butterflies, and naturally enough he made numerous references to the *List* and its author, and to his brother Edward Doubleday. He pointed out the most famous catalogue in earlier years was the one issued in 1776, known as the *Vienna Catalogue*, which was prepared by Denis and Schiffermüller, two officers in the Austrian Army. Their work was particularly important because whereas earlier naturalists, including Linnaeus twenty years before, had quite ignored earlier stages of development when classifying the perfect insect, they had used as their motto 'one eye to the larva and the other to the imago'.

When Doubleday was working on his *List* in 1849 he received a letter from 'his kind and valued friend', M. Achille Guenée who was concerned lest Doubleday should pay too much attention to the classification of lepidoptera in Hübner's *Verzeichniss bekannte Schmetterlinge*; he warned 'Take care then, my dear friend, how you adopt in your catalogue the names from this work and be assured that such an adoption will not be approved by your successors in Entomology'.[83] Doubleday shared his friend's misgivings, but some entomologists looked upon Hübner's work with a less critical eye, and when, a few years after his *List* was first published, J. F. Stephens brought out his *Museum Catalogue*, Doubleday received many letters commenting on the differences in generic names, Stephens having been guided to a large extent by the *Verzeichniss*. 'I cannot understand the love which the English and German Entomologists have suddenly taken for this (Hübner's) senseless work' was Guenée's comment when Doubleday sent him a copy of Stephen's *Catalogue* in January 1851, at the same time pointing out that Hübner had in some cases characterised divisions by colour and marking only, not on structural differences.

Doubleday felt obliged to voice his criticism of Stephen's *Cata-*

31

logue in the *Zoologist*, and this inevitably led to a lengthy correspondence, which was terminated by the editor upon the death of Stephens, then in his 61st year, on 21st December 1852. The argument was pursued with some vigour, in one letter Doubleday writing, in defence of his friends, 'I may say that I am confident that neither M. Guenée nor any of the French naturalists have ever intentionally slighted what has been done in Britain, and I am sure I have ever received the greatest attention and kindness from them.'

After Doubleday had published his *List*, almost every reputable lepidopterist adopted his nomenclature, although a few appeared to oppose it. Stainton (who early in 1850 had presented to the Entomological Society a copy of Doubleday's *List*, showing the several dates of publication on each page), in his *Manual of Entomology* (1856) by not using Doubleday's *List*, brought forth considerable protest from some well-known entomologists, who wrote to the *Zoologist* as follows:—

'We consider Mr. Doubleday's Synonymic List as decidedly the best systematic arrangement, and the one most generally adopted by a large majority of Entomologists of the present day, and we cannot but think that thus tacitly to ignore its existence is greatly to be lamented. We wish it distinctly to be understood that our only motive in requesting the insertion of this protest is to call forth an expression of public opinion from Entomologists in general'.[84]

This letter, signed by C. R. Bree, Herbert Bree, Joseph Greene, and H. Harpur Crewe, apparently caused little surprise, and most readers were content to let the matter rest there.

Guenée and Doubleday worked together closely over many years, the former giving much help to Doubleday, who in turn was able to give valuable advice to Guenée when he compiled his masterly *Histoire naturelle des insectes lépidoptères*. Stainton said his own arrangement of the *Noctuina* in his *Manual*, would follow Guenée's, but in fact, in many instances it did not do so. Undoubtedly much confusion over the nomenclature of this family occurred, as the pages of the *Zoologist* in the 1850's witness, but Harpur Crewe felt sufficiently strongly over Stainton's choice of names that he again protested to the *Zoologist* 'Now I, in common with, I believe, most British Entomologists, look up to Mr. Doubleday as our Mentor, and as I happen to know that it is the opinion of Mr. Doubleday that all other nomenclature must bow before that of M. Guenée . . . .'.

'Surely,' he continued, 'the world-wide reputation and vast experience of M. Guenée, backed as it is by so incontrovertible an authority as Mr. Doubleday, ought to be sufficient to prevent Mr. Stainton from tinkering up anything which comes out of such a workshop.'

Whilst Newman was undoubtedly correct in asserting that the majority of entomologists approved unreservedly Doubleday's *List*, yet from time to time criticism was aired in the scientific magazines. W. A. Lewis read a paper on *Grouping of British Macro-lepidoptera* on 3rd April 1871 at a meeting of the Entomological Society, in which he roundly condemned Doubleday's arrangement, and he followed this up in 1872 by a publication entitled *A discussion of the Law of Priority in entomological literature*: at the same time Lewis attacked Dr. Knagg's *Cabinet List of Lepidoptera of Great Britain and Ireland* and Newman's *Natural History of British Moths*, both recently published. Newman's book was, of course, based on Doubleday's *List*, and in this connection Lewis commented 'Mr. Doubleday having approved certain changes—entomologists want not changes stamped with the approval of this or that leading man, but reasons should be stated and approval left to them'. Knagg's *Cabinet List*, incidentally, was discussed by Doubleday in the *Entomologist* about nine months earlier, with the object of correcting certain errors which were evident to him[85] in the names of some 30 species. Lewis's strictures were delivered about 20 years after Doubleday first published his *List*, and, said Newman, Lewis appeared totally ignorant of the state of nomenclature at that time, and that it became obvious that the *List* was necessary.

'Having been ever since the year 1832 connected with the publication of entomological literature', Newman wrote, 'I was not surprised to hear an appeal from all parts of the country to supply this necessity and as we had then, and have now, but one macro-lepidopterist competent to the task, no one was surprised to hear that I had applied to him for help. To that single macro-lepidopterist all eyes were turned, all voices were in accord, and that man was one of my nearest and dearest friends. A distrust of his own abilities induced a long hesitation and it was only to great pressure that Mr. Doubleday at last yielded: he yielded not because he wanted a list; not because he had any crotchet to air, any purpose to serve, any remuneration to receive, or advantage of any kind to gain; he yielded with the utmost reluctance solely

to oblige one of his oldest friends. He writes on the eve of publication, 'I would not have done this for anyone else; I have done
it entirely to oblige you.'[86]
Newman, as ever, was quick to defend his friend's work, and to a
criticism from entomologists who felt that too much attention had
been paid to the views of their Continental colleagues, he replied
in the *Zoologist*:—
> 'I have often heard my friend Doubleday's arrangement of
> Lepidoptera condemned as "foreign", and so is my own arrange-
> ment and nomenclature of ferns. I totally repudiate all such
> feelings and if I find a Guenée exhibiting a more profound
> knowledge of his subject than a Stephens, a Presl than a Smith,
> I accept their views without any reference to their country. Guenée
> and Presl, like Linnaeus and Cuvier, wrote for the world, why
> should we reckon it a disparagement in being "Foreign"?[87]

R. C. Jordan of Birmingham in writing 'On the origin of British
Lepidoptera', in the *Entomologist's Monthly Magazine* of June 1871,
queried whether the Lepidoptera of the year 2000 would be the same
as those of 1871; after discussing the appearance or disappearance
of several species he concluded 'The changes will probably be few,
and it is consoling to think that the Lepidopterists of a future century
will still be able to refer with satisfaction and profit to Doubleday's
List and Stainton's *Manual*.' It would indeed be interesting to survey
the entomological scene in twenty-five years time, and compare it
with that of 1871, but in view of the ecological disturbances now
taking place, the changes are likely to be far from few, although
important steps are being taken wherever practicable for the preservation of our better-known rarer species.

EDWARD NEWMAN AND EDWARD DOUBLEDAY

Apart from the one very significant work, the *Synonymic List of
British Lepidoptera* which Doubleday published, nothing else of
major importance bore his imprint, although the scientific journals
of his day testify to his prolific correspondence both in their columns,
and to fellow entomologists. His willing assistance and advice to
those who wished to put on more permanent record the results of
their own observations and research were well known. It was his
great friend and fellow Quaker Edward Newman who played a
leading part in the formation and conduct of several of these

34

periodicals, and it would not be out of place therefore to record a few details of the achievements of this contemporary amateur naturalist, who worked so often in close co-operation with Double-day whose outstanding ability and qualities he so clearly recognised.

Newman's main claim to recognition lies in his abounding energy, his courageous and efficient editorship of certain scientific magazines and his excellent books on Ferns, on Butterflies and Moths, which were very thorough, and must have necessitated much research among early and contemporary authors. Until death separated them the Doubleday brothers maintained a close friendship with him from their early youth: he died on 12th June 1876, a year after Henry, with whom he enjoyed a similar reputation for modest living and the simple pleasures of life.

An entomologist, George Samouelle, who became well-known for his *Entomologist's Useful Compendium* and *The Entomological Cabinet*, instituted in 1826 the Entomological Club,[88] which consisted of a small body of 'gentlemen entomologists' who met socially on one evening a month at each other's houses, Newman being an original member. From this Club the *Entomological Magazine* emanated in 1832, of which Newman was appointed its first editor. Although founded in 1826 it was not until ten years later that the printed code laws and bye-laws which subsequently appeared in the *Entomological Magazine*, were formulated, and by this time 100 guineas had been spent on cabinets for specimens. Newman, the Curator, now appealed for assistance in arranging specimens of lepidoptera, diptera, hymenoptera and other insects, and for cata-loguing the library, which included works by Guenée, Fairmaire and many other authors. Edward Doubleday followed the first Curator, Newman, who was in office for more than 10 years, after which Francis Walker was appointed, followed again by Newman. These same people also took a full share in conducting the *Magazine*, for Edward Doubleday, although not an original member of the Club but listed as one in 1832, took over the editorship in 1833 for a year, followed by Francis Walker for a year, when Newman again took up the reins for a year or two until publication was discontinued.

To take the place of this magazine Newman started the *Entomo-logist* in 1840 which ran for two years, when in 1843 it was decided to broaden its appeal by merging it with the *Zoologist*. Newman was its first editor. This magazine he conducted with outstanding success for no less than 33 consecutive years, until his death in 1876. Henry

Doubleday was a subscriber to a testimonial, in the form of a scientific book, presented to Newman in the spring of 1861[89] by a number of *Zoologist* contributors and readers in appreciation of his services.

By 1864 the *Zoologist* had grown rather too bulky and the *Entomologist* was again launched into a separate existence. Up to 1840 Newman gave particular attention to entomology, contributing many articles to both periodicals, and publishing in 1832 an essay entitled *Sphinx Vespiformis* in which he put forward his controversial theory of septenary system in nature. The following year he assisted in the formation of the Entomological Society of London, the year in which he was also elected a Fellow of the Linnean Society. He also found time to publish in 1835 *A Grammar of Entomology*, and then in 1840 his book on *British Ferns*, which ran to a second edition in 1844 and a third ten years later. In 1841 his *Natural History of Insects* was published. This great naturalist with whom the Doubledays had such a close association throughout their lives, undoubtedly had a flair for popular writing, delighting in contributing essays on birds and insects to *Young England* from 1858 to 1861, and was Natural History editor of *The Field* from 1858 to his death in 1876: he also supplied a column or two to each number of the *Friend*, the Quaker journal which was then published monthly, the Natural History section of which he edited.

Probably Newman's best known works today are his *Natural History of British Moths* the last monthly part of which he completed in 1869, and in 1871 he finished *Natural History of British Butterflies*; he was then 70, and it was his last completed work. In passing perhaps one other work should be noted—*The Letters of Rusticus*, a series of essays commenced in 1832, and illustrated by woodcuts after the style of Bewick. For some reason Newman did not wish his name to appear as author and consequently the letters were published under the nom-de-plume of Rusticus; however, it was a secret not very well kept, Newman's son commenting in his *Memoir* after his father's death in 1876 'even Edward Doubleday, his nearest friend and second self, was kept in ignorance of the actual fact, although he, in common with most naturalists, had a shrewd suspicion': however, it was hardly likely that any knowledgeable naturalist was in doubt, as the essays were centred on Godalming, where, it was well known, Newman resided.

He enjoyed the membership of British and foreign scientific clubs and societies, and besides being a member of the Zoological and Linnean, and various botanical Societies, he was President of the Entomological Society of London, and was elected a member of the Imperial Academy of Leopold Charles of Austria, an exclusive Society with a world-wide membership limited to 40 eminent naturalists; Newman never took advantage of the honour to which the latter entitled him, that of prefacing his name with 'Doctor'.

Edward Doubleday who, like his brother Henry, was a bachelor lived from 1811—1849: in spite of his early death, his life was adventurous, and he lived long enough to gain world-wide acknowledgment as an outstanding ornithologist and entomologist, particularly in the philosophical field. 'The glorious time with my lamented friend Edward Doubleday', with 'his varied knowledge and classic lore' was recalled by a friend a few years after Edward's death, when contributing to the *Zoologist* an essay headed by one of Edward's 'numerous ready quotations from Virgil's *Aeneid*'.[90] His paper on *Stygia* which appeared in the *Magazine of Natural History* in 1832 was his first published contribution to Natural History, and the following year he was joint author with Newman of an account of *An Entomological Excursion in North Wales* in the *Entomological Magazine*. He joined with a fellow Quaker named Foster in a trip to the United States of America where he stayed for two years, spending some time at Trenton Falls, and whilst there he collected many specimens of insects, a large number of which were added to the collections in the British and other Museums; upon his return from America he was appointed an official of the British Museum where he stayed until his death in November 1849, and it is said that he brought their collections to a state of great excellence.

He suffered a great disappointment in not being appointed naturalist to the Niger Expedition of 1841,[91] which was supported by the African Civilisation Society, an anti-slavery society sponsored by Prince Albert and others; but perhaps this was fortunate, as the expedition was doomed to failure and abandoned after 41 of the ships' companies of 193 had died of fever.

Had Edward lived longer his name would undoubtedly have found a place beside those of the eminent 19th century entomologists. At the time of his death he was engaged in the production, in parts, *On the Genera of Diurnal Lepidoptera* in collaboration with W. C. Hewitson, who provided the coloured illustrations, and which was to cover all the genera of butterflies. The first part was issued in

November 1846, and the work was proceeding satisfactorily until January 1848, when Edward was obliged to enclose a notice in Part 15, reading:—

'My own ill health, and a severe domestic affliction, having rendered me unable to see through the press the usual amount of text, I am compelled to beg my subscribers to excuse the deficiency which they will find in this, and possibly the next number. Every exertion shall be used to bring the letter-press to a level with the plates as speedily as possible after the part for February.'

Later on, more difficulties arose over the illness of Hewitson, and a note was inserted in Part 21 in 1848, as follows:—

'The authors deeply regret the delay which has occurred in the publication of the present part. It has been caused solely by the severe and long continued illness of Mr. Hewitson, which prevented him putting the last touches to the plates nearly ready at the time of his being suddenly taken ill. Mr. Hewitson's health not being sufficiently restored to enable him to draw the plates, it will be necessary to suspend the work until November by which time measures will be taken to prevent for the future any irregularity in its appearance.'

The domestic affliction to which Edward referred was of course the death of his father in the previous month, and Edward himself died in November 1849. His place was taken by J. O. Westwood who continued with the letterpress, Hewitson carrying on with the plates, of which there were 86, until the final completion of the work in 1852. Although Edward's literary output, like his brother's, was small,[92] it may be mentioned he contributed to Dieffenbach's *Travels in New Zealand*,[93] Stoke's *Discoveries in Australia*, Eyre's *Discoveries in Central Australia* and besides the scientific periodicals mentioned earlier, the *Zoologist, Entomologist*, the *Pharmaceutical Journal* and others, as well as the Proceedings and Transactions of Societies such as the Entomological Society and the Linnean Society. He also compiled the *List of the specimens of Lepidopterous Insects in the Collection of the British Museum*,[94] and published in *Annales de la Société entomologique de France* the *Description de deux nouvelles espèces de charaxes des Indes orientales de la collection de M. Henri Doubleday*.[95] Westwood was the author of the biographical notice in the *Gardener's Chronicle* (to which Edward had frequently contributed), a copy of which he presented to the Entomological Society.

Edward certainly shared his brother Henry's generosity, which this extract from a letter written by Newman to a friend, Jenner Weir, in 1856 illustrates:—

'I am re-arranging the *Lepidoptera* belonging to the Entomological Club and am doing this solely for the purpose of assisting beginners, who are almost daily applying to me for names. I propose being at home at six o'clock every Thursday evening for this special purpose. You will see that the Collection ought to be in better condition than it now is, or I shall not be so useful as I could wish. This idea is not new: I did the same 30 years ago, and continued the practice for many years; but other cares intervened, and the cabinets went to poor *Doubleday*, whose generous disposition was not qualified for a curatorship, and under him the Collection became reduced to a mere skeleton—he gave and lent to everyone whatever they asked of him.'

It was for the last eight years of his life, from 1841—1849 that Edward had care of the Collections of the Entomological Club, and upon his death Newman resumed curatorship; apart from these eight years the Collections were always in Newman's hands.

Enjoying membership of a number of scientific societies, Edward took full advantage of his position in London to keep in touch closely with the latest discoveries and developments, but he was rarely able to see his brother; but whilst Henry was happy to live his life quietly and contentedly in the village of his birth, Edward was ever anxious to see for himself the strange sights which were recalled by travellers on their return from distant countries: the thought of finding in their native haunts the splendid insects to be found there fired his imagination, the American continent in particular having an overwhelming fascination for him.

At a meeting of the Entomological Club, reported in the *Entomological Magazine* for July 1835, when discussing the evidence for the luminosity of the South American Lantern Fly, *Fulgora lanternaria*, he spoke effusively of his desires, which were shortly to be fulfilled, in the following words:—

'. . . but yet sometimes, in my solitary wanderings through our forest, or whilst I rest myself on the stump of some old oak tree, my imagination calls up to my view the splendid scenery of tropical America, her vast rivers, her snowy mountains, her groves of palms, of *Lecythis*, of *Cavanilleria*, and a thousand other magnificent trees, intertwined by *Paulini, Banisteriae, Passiflorae,* and *Bignoniae*, with blue, crimson or golden blossoms, from which

the humming-bird now pecks the tiny insect, now darts from them through the air,
"Like winged flowers, or flying gems"
and then a voice seems to whisper to me, such lands must thou visit—such scenes wilt thou find displayed before thee. O that these visions may be realised! O that they may not be a mere mirage of a mind enthusiastic solely on one subject!'[96]

ON BOTANICAL MATTERS, AND HENRY DOUBLEDAY'S SKILFUL
ASSISTANT JAMES ENGLISH, THE FUNGUS EXPERT

The great John Ray (1627—1704/5), the 'Father of Botany' in this country was a priest of the Church of England who, with many other conscientious clergy, was forced by Charles' Act of Uniformity to resign his living. The account of his life and how he, the son of a blacksmith at Black Notley in Essex rose to great eminence, is so well known that it will not be repeated here: suffice it to say that the great scientific works which came from his pen would not have been written had he not made his firm stand against an unjust law. Although Ray lived rather too early to have known the many Quaker botanists who flourished in the 18th century, yet it is known he was particularly friendly with Thomas Lawson (1630—1691),[97] known as 'the first Quaker botanist', who also was a former minister, of Rampside in Lancashire. Lawson who 'travelled in the Quaker Ministry', knew most of the botanists in the Royal Society, and was apparently of much service to Ray to whom he sent many specimens of plants collected on his journeys, mostly from the northern English counties; one letter to Ray is of particular importance in that it enumerates, with localities, about 150 species of plants which he found chiefly in Westmoreland and adjacent counties: this letter was written from Great Strickland on 9th April 1688. Ray praised him as 'an industrious diligent and skilful botanist' in the preface to his book *Synopsis methodica stirpium Britannicarum*, published in 1690.

In addition to his botanical work Ray's entomological studies were of great importance; however, it was a pity that Doubleday, who had the galaxy of Quaker botanists of the previous century to encourage him,[98] was not more familiar with Ray's masterpieces, which were of great influence to Linnaeus and Buffon: admittedly, Ray wrote in Latin, but the Doubleday brothers were not unacquainted with the language, which as previously mentioned, was almost essential for

40

any scientific pursuit: for example the 'excellent Mr. Ray' as Gilbert White called him, had no doubt in his mind that *Primula elatior*, the true Oxlip, was a species quite distinct from the other two members of this family, the Primrose (*P. vulgaris*) and the Cowslip (*P. veris*), which occur in the Doubledays' home county, Essex, and in adjoining Cambridgeshire. Ray in his first published botanical work, *Catalogus Plantarum circa Cantabrigiam nascentium*, 1660, noted these three species, which he named *Primula veris elatior pallido flore*, the Great Cowslip or Oxlips, *Primula veris vulgaris*, the Common Primrose, and *Primula veris major*, Paigles or Cowslips, all as growing abundantly so that the vast amount of research and the discovery of what was thought to be a new British species by Doubleday in Essex, all seem directed towards a confirmation of what in fact the great botanist had already observed. It was in the 1840's of last century that a great deal of experiment and discussion took place on whether *elatior* was a true species, and although opinion seemed fairly evenly divided for a time, in the end the evidence was overwhelmingly in favour and Doubleday's conclusion that it was distinct was proved correct.[99] Edward Doubleday, speaking at a London Botanical Society meeting, gave evidence that Henry 'had examined thousands of plants at and near Bardfield and never observed a single instance of a solitary flower being thrown up as in the hybrid', and Miller Christy confirmed, many years afterwards that Doubleday had cultivated the species for more than a quarter of a century, detecting no change in the form of the plant. Darwin too carried out much research, setting out clearly the steps by which he reached the same conclusion, in *Forms of Flowers*,[100] the first chapters of which are concerned with Primulas.

Doubleday's own interest in the plant was kindled by discovering it growing in Essex in 1842, a fact recorded in the *Phytologist* and recalled by Miller Christy in a paper read to the Essex Field Club in 1882.[101] These were his words:—

'The account of the first discovery of *Primula elatior* in Britain may be found in the early volumes of the *Phytologist*. To Henry Doubleday, our distinguished Essex naturalist, belongs the honour of having first recognised it in this country, he having found it in the meadows beside the river at Great Bardfield, at which place, as I have reason to know, he frequently visited his first-cousin, the late Richard Smith. He recorded this fact in the *Phytologist* (Vol. I p. 204) on 20th.4.42.'

It is now clear that the laborious work undertaken by Doubleday and many contemporary botanists was extremely valuable in providing the proof which ended the long controversy, yet the credit for first identifying *elatior* as a British plant cannot be claimed entirely for the Epping naturalist, as so many writers over the years have done.

At the meeting mentioned above, Miller Christy's talk was illustrated by James English with species of the *Primula* genus, preserved by his 'own process'. James Lake English, a founder member of the Essex Field Club, spent many years in Doubleday's employment as a collector and assistant, the two naturalists working in close co-operation. A short notice of how this arose and of English's own skills follows.

He was born on 21st August 1820 in the Epping cottage in which nearly all his life was spent. His father who was a gardener, having been earlier a soldier in the Dragoon Guards had, so far as we know, but little interest in entomology, although his son may well have inherited his enthusiasm for botany from him. It was fortunate that his father decided to settle down in that quiet little country town and the natural bent of the boy became clear when his father died in 1836: previous to this, after some education at Palmer's School at Epping, he had assisted his father, but now, being thrown upon his own resources, he started collecting insects for the boys at the Friends' School at Epping, which the Doubleday boys had earlier attended, and so became well known to Henry.

James Lake English's mechanical genius was also great, as was his skill in the culture of plants. Miller Christy, author of several books relating to Essex, informs us that English constructed a lathe with which he turned out excellent work in wood and metal, and that he made a compound microscope, using it constantly for many years in his botanical observations. After the death of Doubleday in 1875, English maintained himself by working as a general mechanic and taxidermist, and any tool required was at once contrived and made by him.

Much business was brought to English because of his skill as a preserver of birds and animals, and he greatly improved many processes, resulting in hundreds of specimens of his work in taxidermy being found in country houses in Essex and elsewhere, as well as in many museums. The Museum of the Essex Field Club benefited in particular from his presentations, or from work carried out for them by English, such as the example shown in the following extract from a Meeting report dated 25th November 1882:—'Mr. G. P. Hope sent two specimens of the Golden-Eyed Garrot and one of the Red-Necked Grebe in the flesh, which were placed in Mr. English's hands for preservation.'

Had his education and early environment been more favourable he would undoubtedly have achieved high eminence as a naturalist, as it was, English did some very useful work, but unfortunately he left few records of his observations. Besides being well-known as a practical field-student of cryptogamic botany and a lepidopterist, his knowledge of birds and his skilful taxidermy entitle him to a high place among Essex ornithologists. He died on January 12th 1888 in the cottage in which he first saw the light; upon his death his collections were sold and his cabinet of lepidoptera was purchased by Mr. T. J. Mann of Hyde Hall, Sawbridgeworth, reputedly for the sum of £100. A member of the Church of England, he was buried in the churchyard of Epping Old Church.

There is no doubt that English served Doubleday well, receiving in turn a training which was of incalculable value. He also gained a wide reputation for skill in preserving fungi,[102] and for identifying the many species to be found in Epping Forest, publishing jointly with Dr. Cooke the *Preliminary List of the Hymenomycetal Fungi of Epping Forest*; he was the first to discover in England the fungus *Polyporus umbellatus*. A year or two before his death he spent a good deal of time in the study of mosses, in 1885 commencing the publication of *Fasciculi of Epping Forest Mosses*, of which five parts appeared.

Epping also produced another very competent but little-known botanist, a namesake of the illustrious John Ray, who lived 150 years earlier. From the herbarium of this later John Ray, one hundred and fifty one specimens from Epping went towards the collection of dried plants made by Miss Doubleday of Halstead, who died towards the end of the nineteenth century. The whole collection in which two hundred specimens of Essex plants were included and which was well cared for, fell 'by a series of happy circumstances,' into the hands of W. M. Webb, as he mentioned in a notice in the *Essex Naturalist* of 1900.[103] Gibson, in his *Flora of Essex*, made reference to his contemporary, John Ray, formerly of Epping, but observed that his list of plants was mostly included in Henry Doubleday's.

In 1841 the attention of botanists was drawn by Henry Doubleday to two rare plants which he found in Essex, the first was *Lilium martagon*[104] which was shown him by his cousin Richard Smith of Great Bardfield, where it was found to be growing plentifully on the road between Great Bardfield and Saffron Walden; and a year later, he reported *Lavatera olbia*, the Tree Mallow, growing at Fairmead Bottom in the Forest. In 1838 and 1839 the road through Epping Forest to Woodford was under construction and in the earth that was thrown up from the Forest hundreds of plants of this species appeared, flourished and flowered: a few years later, however, they had almost disappeared, as the grass was then growing over.[105] Newman commented[106] that he knew of no other location for the Tree Mallow, which is really at home only on the Mediterranean coast.

Although as a botanist Henry Doubleday cannot be regarded as anything more than a careful observer nevertheless his findings were invariably of some value and interest to fellow naturalists: the cultivation of his garden became, in his later years, one of his chief occupations, and he achieved excellent results in his kitchen garden, with strawberries in particular: 'we shrewdly suspect that some of his numerous friends contrived to fix the period of the visits in the strawberry season' said the *Entomologists' Monthly Magazine* in his obituary notice. Many were the prizes he took for this fruit, upon which he clearly became an authority. His letter to the *Gardener's Chronicle* in 1862 on the Filbert Pine Strawberry was quoted by Darwin in *The Variation of Animals and Plants under Domestication*: 'this strawberry' Doubleday commented 'requires more water than any other variety; and if the plants once suffer from drought, they will do little or no good afterwards.'

The *Phytologist* and magazines such as the *Gardener's Chronicle* received many letters and reports from the Doubledays over the years, and Edward was a member of the Council of the Botanical Society of London, to which they made frequent gifts of specimens of local plants.

OBSERVATIONS ON SOME UNUSUAL SPECIES OF MOTHS

Most of Doubleday's leisure time throughout his life, and it must be remembered that he was an amateur entomologist in an age before professionalism generated the scientific advancements which we now take for granted, was spent in observing and classifying lepidoptera,

44

mainly *heterocera*, the moths, upon which he was able to direct his critical faculties, long before the more recent methods of genitalia examination under the microscope became the most dependable and accurate means of identification. For a time he devoted much trouble to the small delicately patterned family of moths, the *Eupitheciae*— the Pugs, for which he can be given the credit of discovering and naming several new species. As usual, opinions were sought of those lepidopterists for whom he had high regard, and rarely did they differ from his own. Guenée for example received in 1858 a specimen of a Pug from Doubleday which was apparently new to science, named by the Epping naturalist *E. viminata*, the insect frequenting osier beds, as the name implies;[107] for this Guenée gave immediate acquiescence. Doubleday also sent about the same time an unidentified Pug which was recognised by Guenée as *E. helveticaria*, a moth usually found in Switzerland: larvae from which this insect was bred were found on juniper by an entomologist named Logan,[108] and drawings made of them by Harpur Crewe, which were shown, together with those of *E. tripunctata* and *E. trisignaria*, at an Entomological Society meeting by Dr. Knaggs.

Notes on little-known British Eupitheciae was the title of an article contributed by Doubleday to the *Zoologist* in 1861,[109] being a corollary of his long essay of five or six pages which gave a full register, in the same journal some five years earlier. In order to obtain the co-operation and considered opinion of the foremost experts in the world for the compilation of this little monograph, he sent to his 'kind friend, M. Guenée' all the British Pug species he could find for his careful examination; and borrowed from Stainton certain entomological books which he did not possess such as those by Hübner and Herrich-Schäffer; Edwin Shepherd and Bond also assisted in the painstaking examination of many specimens, embracing about 40 species.[110]

We don't know whether these small and fragile moths suffered any damage in transit on their perilous journeys to the Continent; Doubleday does not disclose that they ever came to harm, but bearing in mind his sharp criticism of those who sent specimens through the post inadequately packed, we can be sure that every possible precaution against harm was taken.

Whilst a complete catalogue of the scarce insects which Doubleday collected from the Epping area by his own hand or with the help of James English or other local residents, would be tedious and outside

45

the scope of this little record, perhaps it would not be out of place to mention some of the more interesting insects which he was fortunate enough to have encountered. The references may be consulted for those wishing for rather more information, but a glance through the next few paragraphs will show how fortunate he was in meeting with species for which we may now search a whole lifetime in vain.

For example, the rare moth for which many generations of collectors, having taken the hint from Stainton's *Manual*, searched the stubble fields in vain, was the Crimson Speckled Footman (*Lithosia pulchella*) yet Doubleday had a splendid specimen brought to him at Epping in 1846.[111] Newman in *British Moths* (1869) said 'we believe there are two or three other British specimens in different cabinets.'[112] Several of this attractive family of 'Footmen' (*Lithosiae*) are uncommon, some species closely resembling others, and Doubleday clearly spent much time in trying to identify and distinguish between them: he was the first to determine the Pigmy Footman (*L. pygmaeola*)[113] and to identify another Footman, the Hoary (*L. caniola*), not previously recognised in this country, although common on the Continent: the circumstances of this were as follows:—[114]

'Mr. King of Torquay, called upon me a few weeks since with some insects collected in Devon and Cornwall, from which I picked out a worn specimen of a *Lithosia* which appeared distinct from any recorded British species: I believe it to be *L. caniola* of *Hübner*, etc.—a species not uncommon in France, and very likely to occur here. Mr. Barrett took four specimens of the same species in Ireland last August, one of which he kindly sent me to examine. Although in much better condition than the one which I have, it is not fine; but I think there can be little doubt of its being *L. caniola*,[115] a species likely to be overlooked from its dull colour, which would lead many to consider it one of the common species in faded condition. My friend, M. Guenée, who has all my *Lithosiae* for examination, has just sent a paper upon the European species of the genus *Lithosia* for publication in the *Transactions* of the Entomological Society of France; as soon as it appears I will send a few remarks upon the British species for insertion in the *Zoologist*.'[116]

A full description of the larva and moth of the species *Zygaena meliloti*, known as the New Forest Burnet, now supposed to be extinct in this country, although it is well distributed in Europe, was given by Doubleday to the *Entomologist* in 1872, and this was of great interest, as it had never before been found in Britain. This pretty little moth was found by several collectors about this time in the New Forest, Hampshire, and five specimens were examined by Doubleday. They were sent to him by a friend, on behalf of the captor, E. Harper, for his judgement on them, and Doubleday whose advice on this family, the 'Burnets' was frequently sought at once identified them as the continental species; this insect is very similar in colouring and marking to *Z. trifolii*, the Five-spot Burnet, and Harper felt that possibly his insects were small varieties of that moth. The following year, *Z. trifolii* together with *Z. lonicerae* (the analogous Narrow-bordered Five-Spot Burnet) were described at length, and the localities where they could be found mentioned by Doubleday in the *Entomologist*, at the request of Edward Newman. Of *lonicerae* he said:—'I have bred many hundred specimens of the perfect insect from larvae obtained in this locality . . .' (Epping).[117]

On one occasion he sent a larva of a Scandinavian variety of this family, *Z. exulans* (*var. vanadis* (Dalman))[118] to Newman who described it minutely together with the moth, in the *Entomologist*. The larva, he said, was in his possession 'through the unremitting kindness of Mr. Doubleday'', and the moth, which was identified by Doubleday, was one of several caught at Braemar by Dr. Buchanan White and Mr. Traill. White had sent some to Doubleday for his opinion.[119]

A particularly exciting capture occurred on 29th June 1845, and one which created great interest in entomological circles. Doubleday was walking with a friend through a heathy part of Epping Forest when he saw several specimens of a pretty moth, which he identified as the Rosy Marbled Moth (*Erastria venustula*), on ferns. He caught two of them with pill boxes, but returning the next day could find no trace of them.[120] He was told by another collector, Mr. Bentley, that his father caught this insect in the Forest more than 40 years before (i.e. about the year 1800), but no record seems to have been made of this, or of any capture previous to Doubleday's. Newman in 1869[121] records only Doubleday as finding it up to that date, but further research[122] has shown that although no capture appears to have been made between 1845 and 1858, it was taken at Loughton, Essex and in Epping Forest in 1858 and 1859; and in fact between 1858 and 1921 nearly 40 records of this little moth were made, all in localities at Epping, Loughton and Brentwood, where it persisted until recent times. It is occasionally found in other southern counties, but very rarely, so that this scarce little insect is still almost confined to one or two stations in Essex.[123]

Ongar Park Wood was the first location in this country where specimens of the Dusky Marbled Brown moth (*Glaphisia crenata*) were found in 1839[124] and 1841: both insects, females, were taken by Doubleday. South, in *Moths of the British Isles* could record only three examples including these two.

The *Victoria County History of Essex* (1) 1903, gives Doubleday as its reference on frequent occasions, some of the more interesting of which are noted here from time to time; he is named as the discoverer of the Dusky Clearwing (*Sesia tabaniformis*) in Essex, the only record to that date being the one he found at Epping in 1839. A moth of an allied family, the rare and local Narrow-bordered Bee Hawk he also took at Epping, only two other Essex localities being recorded.

ON HIBERNATION AND OTHER PROBLEMS

The 19th Century witnessed the formation of many clubs and societies devoted to the study of natural sciences, and the spirit of enquiry thus engendered spread through all classes of society. The discovery of a species of insect new to science, or of one not previously found in this country, is today a memorable event, but in Doubleday's time it was of frequent occurrence. It must be recognised that for his generation he was outstanding so far as British macrolepidoptera were concerned, and references to his discoveries although only touched upon here, are to those made by an exceptional man, yet they play but a minor part when viewed in the light of the total rapid advancement of entomological science in his time. An examination of the scientific literature from 1830 onwards would reveal many more citations, and the contents of his voluminous correspondence, had it been preserved, and his diary which was lost, would have been most illuminating. Although Doubleday shared in the discussions on controversial issues brought into print by fellow entomologists, such as whether the Brimstone Butterfly (*G. rhamni*) is double-brooded[125]—the subject of much correspondence in the *Zoologist* in 1855 (Doubleday was of the opinion that it was univoltine), yet it seemed that only after persuasion would he publish the results of his experience, perhaps assuming that other entomologists already had that knowledge. C. R. Bree, during the course of this correspondence referred to the hibernation of certain insects as 'casual' or 'accidental' to which Doubleday emphasizing that this is not so, reluctantly replied ('I had no wish to say anything more about *G. rhamni*, but I seem almost compelled to reply to Mr. C. R. Bree . . .'):—

'Last winter some large stacks of beech faggots, which had been loosely stacked up in our forest the preceding spring, with the dead leaves adhering to them, were taken down and carted away, and among these were many scores of *Io*, *Urticae*, and *Polychloros*. Any mild day in the middle of winter, if you take a pair of fumigating bellows and blow tobacco smoke into furze bushes, you will drive out scores of *Depressariae*,[126] etc. which are hibernating there.' . . . To which Bree, in conclusion, commented:—

'If there is one thing more than another which I have been impressed with by the late discussion, it is the fact that there is a great deal of knowledge stored up in the minds of naturalists of the present day, as securely as their own cabinets are protected from the investigating propensities of *Acari* or *Dermestes*. I think his (Doubleday's) opinion at all times valuable, and especially so on all points connected with lepidoptera.'[127]

Some discussion arose in the *Zoologist* in 1852 after the attention of the Entomological Society had been drawn by Mr. Douglas to the finding of insects impaled on thorns or sharp wire. Butcher-birds, it was decided, were probably responsible, but Douglas, not satisfied, referred the occurrence to Doubleday, who informed him that he had seen a specimen of the Shoulder-striped Wainscot[128] (*Leucania comma*) transfixed by a spine of dry furze, which had been placed on the top of a garden wall to keep cats away. The head of the moth, said Doubleday, was *towards* the spine, as if its flight had been suddenly arrested; and many years after this in 1873 Mr. Meldola showed a *noctua* which had been impaled on a thorn, to an Entomological Society meeting. The general opinion was that it was the work of a shrike, although views were also expressed that insects may be impaled by other means.

In the *Entomologist* for the same year, 1873, Newman apparently became rather exasperated by Doubleday's reluctance to discuss the *Acentropus* genus (aquatic Pyralid moths) about which information appeared to be scanty. In an attempt to draw him out, Newman wrote:—

'What are the affinities of the *Acentropus*? When I consider the position occupied by Mr. Doubleday among living entomologists, and the universal respect in which his judgement is held, not simply among ourselves in England, but also on the continent of Europe and in America, it is much to be desired that he would express his views. Beyond the fact that the genus *Acentropus* is not to be found in either Edition of his invaluable *Synonymic List*, we have no indication of Mr. Doubleday's opinion. The same may be said of M. Guenée, whose abstention from the discussion is equally to be lamented.'

ON MORE RARE MOTHS

The rare fenland moth, the Reed Leopard (*Zeuzera arundinis*) was noted by Doubleday as emerging from the pupa at 10 o'clock at night, when he commented on its profusion at Whittlesea Mere in 1850:[129] in that year too it was abundant in Holme Fen, near Yaxley in Huntingdonshire where many years earlier he had taken it—'I discovered a male specimen of this singular species floating in a ditch in Holme Fen, some years since' he wrote in 1848,[130] in which year two female specimens were taken near the same spot, one of which went to Doubleday, and the other to his friend Thomas Allis, of York.[131]

Another moth, first found in Ranworth Fen was *Sericoris doubledayana* (The Fen Marble), so named by C. G. Barrett, who described it in the *Entomologist's Monthly Magazine* in 1872. He wrote from Norwich on 12th February:—

'It gives me particular pleasure to name this novelty in honour of my kind friend, Mr. Doubleday, who has spent so many years in elucidating the history and clearing up the nomenclature of our native lepidoptera.'

The several thousand species of British moths, compared with the three score odd number of butterflies, provided Doubleday with great scope for his research, and it was in the study of these, the *heterocera*, that he excelled, especially in the *Noctuas*, which are the large-bodied, fast-flying moths, and of the *Geometers*, the slender-bodied, large-winged moths, the caterpillars of which are familiarly known as 'loopers'.

To many people it is undoubtedly the hawk-moths which attract most attention, due to their striking colours and large size. They have narrow pointed wings and are rapid fliers, similar to the birds from which they are named. In Britain there are only a dozen or so representatives of this family, and Doubleday did not neglect them when the occasion arose; but one feels that his study of this family was only incidental—probably the ease with which they can be identified and the rarity of variations soon satisfied Doubleday's enquiring mind, although he was always eager to record the appearance of the rarer species.

None of the hawk-moths is very common and some are extremely rare; others are local in distribution and their numbers vary considerably from year to year, chiefly because, being strong on the wing, many migrate from the continent, and these vary according to the season. Of these popular moths perhaps the species best known although scarce, is the Death's Head Hawk-moth, one of our largest English moths, and reputedly the only one able to make a sound, albeit only a faint squeak, in all stages of its existence after hatching from the egg, i.e. as a larva, pupa and imago. Doubleday forwarded to the *Zoologist* in 1846 his observations on this handsome insect, which many years later he was breeding successfully—he recorded that three moths, two females and one male, emerged from his pupae on 16th September 1865.[132]

A few days before he gave this information to the *Zoologist* he reported that he had captured the incredible number of over 40 Convolvulus Hawk Moths over three or four petunias, in mid-August. That year saw the immigration of large numbers of this rare and spendid insect, and those caught by Doubleday undoubtedly were of European origin. Judged by the wing span alone, it is our largest moth, even exceeding the Death's Head Hawk, and it must have been a magnificent sight to see them hovering over the flowers, extending the proboscis, which is three times the length of the body. The larva of this huge moth is rarely found in Britain, and a correspondent wrote to the *Entomologist* in 1873 asking for a description of the caterpillar and its food plant; Doubleday in a very long letter in reply quoted Boisduval's full description of the larva and its food, and went on to say, 'My friend M. Constant says *S. convolvuli* is commoner at Autun than *S. ligustri*' (Privet-hawk—not uncommon in England). Doubleday himself was fortunate enough to have had one brought to him, together with some Death's

Head larvae, 'some years ago' (written in 1873), and also another, with no date given, which was found on a garden hedge overgrown with *Convolvulus sepium*, upon which the insect had undoubtedly been feeding. Two years after Doubleday had written this, and a few months after his death, it was reported[133] that numerous captures of the Convolvulus Hawk Moth had been made in that year (1875), and several females taken which had contained no eggs. No reason for this was advanced, and Newman remarked that Doubleday had made a similar observation with regard to our larger Hawk-moths, particularly the Death's Head, many years before.[134]

The first specimen of the rare Silver-striped Hawk moth was reputed to have been found in 1779 in Bunhill Fields Burial Ground in London, and that insect found a home in the collection of A. H. Haworth. Instances of the occurrence of this beautiful European migrant are recorded from time to time, and sometimes the larva is found. In 1865[135] the caterpillar was found in an Epping garden, and brought to Doubleday on October 7th; three days later he reported that it was changing into a pupa, although whether the moth was bred successfully is not known. Richard South in *Moths of the British Isles* may have been in error in giving October 1867 as the date of this incident.

GUENEEI, ASHWORTHII, AND BARRETTII

Doubleday appeared to be particularly busy in his correspondence with fellow lepidopterists concerning identification problems, during the two decades from 1830 to 1850, and the number of species which were new or first recorded in Britain over this period was indeed remarkable. Sometimes the capture of such an insect was publicised through the medium of a scientific journal by the finder, but in many cases it was left to Doubleday to announce the event, and it consequently fell to him to be the author of several species, one of which he named after his closest friend, Achille Guenée. This was a moth which Guenée had in his collection in France, labelled as a variety of the Flounced Rustic (*Luperina testacea*), but it was not until Doubleday had emphasized that in his opinion it was a new species and sent him a specimen from England, collected by the Rev. Burnley, that he concurred with Doubleday, who consequently named it *Luperina gueneei*,[136] Guenée's Sandhill Rustic.

Agrotis ashworthii, Ashworth's Rustic was the name bestowed by

Doubleday on the moth first taken at Llangollen by Joseph Ashworth in 1853; again, Guenée was asked to confirm his opinion that it was new to science, and he did this after Doubleday had sent him a male specimen to examine, and a drawing of the female.[137] Another moth, Barrett's Marbled Coronet, was named after its discoverer C. G. Barrett, who found it at Howth in Ireland in June 1861: Doubleday named it *Dianthoecia barrettii*:[138] he also identified a moth of the same family which Barrett had caught on the coast near Dublin in 1860 as the scarce Pod-lover (*Dianthoecia capsophila*).[139]

ATTEMPTS AT NATURALISATION

We read occasionally of naturalists trying to acclimatize some of our rarer, or even foreign species in certain English localities, and Doubleday certainly tried to introduce a number of scarce insects into the neighbourhood of Epping: but it was extremely unlikely that he attempted to stock the locality with the beautiful Continental butterfly, the Apollo, as a correspondent to the *Entomologist* suggested,[140] the implication being made in a letter by George Box Holmes of Alton, dated 6th February 1872, to Newman:—

'Doritis Apollo at Epping—

I see, at the end of your volume on Butterflies, that you have not seen an authenticated specimen of Doritis Apollo caught in this country. You will be pleased to learn that I have one in my possession, which was taken by my late son at Epping, about the year 1847 or 1848, at the time he was a pupil at Dr. Usmar's school, which was previously that of Isaac Payne, where I was also a scholar for 6 years, and part of the time with Henry and Edward Doubleday. It is possible that Henry Doubleday may have attempted to stock the neighbourhood with some of the rarer butterflies and moths. I think I have heard my son say so, but am not quite certain.'

This drew a reply from Henry Doubleday, to whom the letter was immediately forwarded by Newman, to the effect that there must have been a mistake in the supposition that it was taken at Epping, Newman adding that he still thought that no authenticated British specimen existed. This notification of such a rare lepidopteron was correctly referred to as an error in *The Lepidoptera of Essex* (1890)[141] by E. D. W. Fitch, a catalogue of published records which listed 55 butterflies in Essex out of the 65 British species. This list contains, naturally, numerous other references to the Doubledays.

It is certain, however, that Henry Doubleday did attempt to naturalize the Swallowtail Butterfly, now confined to the area of the Fens, but that experiment was unsuccessful, as it was with the attempts of so many other entomologists. He turned out many of these handsome insects in the Epping Forest district in the years 1848 to 1850,[142] but they failed to establish themselves; being of a painstaking nature he would have checked that all the obvious requirements for making it a success were present, but too often there are factors at which only guesses may be made which doom such experiments to failure.

Many years later[143] Professor R. Meldola wrote to the *Entomologist* of his equally unsuccessful attempt to colonise this butterfly near Dunmow, in Essex in 1909, on the Duke of Warwick's estate. The Swallowtail once had a much larger area of distribution; Newman, for example, mentioned finding the caterpillars feeding on rue at Tottenham, where he was a schoolboy; this was probably just before 1812. A surgeon named Gutteridge of Maldon in Essex, recorded the capture of a Swallowtail there early in August, 1872, and many other examples could be quoted showing the wide distribution, its capture in Kent and Sussex being particularly frequent. We know that from time to time Doubleday bred large numbers of this butterfly: for example in 1854 he had about 100 pupae in the same cage, the first butterflies appearing in May and the last in the first week in September, but he was never successful in rearing a butterfly from a larva in the same season.[144]

In 1839 Doubleday found the larvae of the Gipsy Moth, *Liparis dispar*, swarming in Yaxley Fen, but whether he tried to get a colony established in Epping is not known, but we do know that on his trip to Paris in 1843 he found time to collect a large quantity of pupae which he brought back to Epping. The imagines successfully emerged, and the following spring he turned out thousands of larvae which he had bred. Perhaps it was as well they did not establish themselves, although he saw plenty of moths in one field the following August, for the insect is sometimes very destructive to trees, in both the Old and New Worlds. He made one further attempt to colonise it, but with no more success; James English had found the larvae quite common but not abundant in Yaxley Fen in 1845 and from moths obtained he bred more larvae which he released:—

'In 1846 I obtained an immense quantity of eggs from moths bred from larvae brought from Yaxley. Next Spring great numbers of larvae were turned out on the dwarf sallows growing among the gravel-pits in the Forest. A few larvae were seen the following year, but not afterwards.'[145]

The slight difference between French examples of the moth and our own Fenland insect was noticed by Doubleday who concluded that specimens found in old English collections were probably all foreign. There is no doubt that he was very puzzled by the fact that the moth frequents towns and suburban gardens on the Continent, but here it is almost confined to fenland areas.

Another experiment, which had little chance of success from the outset, was the releasing of a number of specimens of the Great Emperor Moth (*Saturnia* (*Pavonia*) *major*) which he had bred from ova sent to him from America, probably by his brother Edward. After that season no specimens were seen, but a number of people, recognising the unusual species, captured some of them and brought them to Doubleday to identify or purchase. They were probably disappointed and perhaps not a little irritated to learn that he was responsible for their appearance.[146]

Scarlet Tiger Moths were also bred and released by Doubleday over the same period that he experimented with the Swallowtail Butterflies, but with similar results:[147] he also bred the Striped Tiger Moth, an extremely rare insect in England, Newman remarking in the *Entomologist*[148] 'through the kindness of my friend, Mr. Double-day, I have the opportunity of describing a full-fed caterpillar'; whether Doubleday tried to acclimatize this species as well is not known.

By his success in breeding lepidoptera Doubleday was able on a number of occasions to settle queries regarding certain species of moths which some lepidopterists regarded as distinct, and others only variations, such as *Miana strigilis* (Marbled Minor) and *M. aethiops*,[149] and he made clear that the different imagines of *Selenia illuniaria*, the Early Thorn Moth, which emerge in April and July, are but seasonal dimorphs, not separate species which many eminent entomologists, including Haworth in *Lepidoptera Britannica*, thought to be the case.[150]

It is said the draining of the Fens was partly responsible for the disappearance of the Large Copper butterfly, which became extinct over 100 years ago. Newman in his *Natural History of British Butterflies* noted that its latest capture was thought to be 1847 or 1848 at Yaxley or Holm Fens, and at that date (1871) was believed extinct. He mentions however—'My acquaintance with the caterpillar and chrysalis was made very many years ago in Mr. Doubleday's garden at Epping, where the very plant *Rumex hydrolapathum* on which the caterpillar fed is still in existence.'

A few years before the last reported capture of this insect, perhaps even after that date, in view of his well known reluctance to publish his observations, Doubleday was successfully breeding this rapidly disappearing species in his garden, and some striking varieties were obtained, as the following extract from Frohawk's *Varieties of British Butterflies* (1938) demonstrates:—

'*Aberration:* A few striking aberrations of this fine insect are in existence. In the Doubleday collection in the British Museum is a female specimen with a black wedge-shaped blotch at the base of each forewing, also a male with some additional spots in the forewing. In the Lord Rothschild Collection is a male aberration, with large, whitish, wedge-shaped blotches running from the outer margins of the forewings towards the base and lunular whitish marks on the hind wings. Both this and the two in the British Museum of Natural History were bred by Doubleday in his garden at Epping in 1842.[151] In the Dale collection at Oxford is an almost entirely black female. It is probable that this species was liable to considerable aberration, for about a century ago little attention was given to aberrant specimens of lepidoptera.'

In 1884, some years after Doubleday's death, James L. English gave an address[152] to the Essex Field Club, entitled *Entomological Notes from an Old Pocket Book*, the period covered by the talk being 1838 to 1862. In it he gave details of localities of many rare species which he had found near Epping during those years, but he said that in 1846 he stayed at Yaxley in the Huntingdon fen district. 'I was also delighted to catch three large Copper butterflies, *Polyommatus dispar*, the last specimens, I believe, of that grand and long-lost species ever taken in Britain.'

Now and again controversial points were raised in connection with the identity or habits of rare butterflies, and it was usually on these occasions when Doubleday was encouraged to give his opinions, which were always worth while and respected.

In 1875, S. L. Mosley wrote to the *Entomologist* saying that he had taken the rare Wood White butterfly in the New Forest without the usual black tips to the wings. Newman's *Natural History of British Butterflies* had been published a few years earlier, depicting a similar insect as the usual form of the female, but as other entomologists took the view that it was a variety, Mosley asked for further advice. Upon receipt of this letter Newman asked three eminent lepidopterists for their opinions: they were Doubleday, Birchall, and Weir. It is not clear what the others thought of it, but it had the effect of attracting a letter from Doubleday in which the various European types were described, together with a description of the New Forest and Tilgate Forest specimens. He said he had never seen a British female of the type from those localities, but he had Sicilian specimens, given to him by M. Bellier de la Chavignerie, which were pure white on both surfaces, without any markings, thus implying that Newman was correct, although Mosley, in thanking Doubleday for his information, still admitted feeling doubtful. Actually the female of the British race of this uncommon species shows practically no black, and the females of some varieties are quite devoid of markings, and it is just possible that it may have been one of these which Mosley took. The Wood White occurs now only in the South of England and then but rarely, and in parts of Ireland. Early in this century it disappeared from the New Forest and Tilgate Forest, and may not have returned, over-collecting and natural causes possibly being responsible for its disappearance from these areas. James English recorded its occurrence freely near Epping in 1839, but Doubleday makes no mention of this, and it has been noticed in Essex since then on very few occasions only.[153]

The pages of the *Entomologist* for the years 1870, 1871 and 1874 contain much interesting material concerning the identity of a number of species of Fritillaries, mostly rare, which had been taken, or were alleged to have been taken in this country. The discussion was mainly between Bond, the Rev. W. Hambrough, Doubleday, A. G. Butler of the British Museum, Newman, Parry, Wigan, Gregson and others, and revolved chiefly around the identification of insects such as *Argynnis niobe*, *A. aglaia* (Dark Green Fritillary) and *A. adippe* (High Brown Fritillary), and considerable exchange of specimens took place.

The argument centred chiefly over whether *niobe* was a separate species from *adippe*, or whether the butterflies were varieties of either. Doubleday had no doubt whatever that the species were distinct, and that the insects he examined were *niobe*. They surely were, but as the sources from which they came were not entirely trustworthy, he would have been justified in questioning further the circumstances of their capture especially when such collectors as Parry and Wigan were involved.

It was Edward Doubleday who found the Heath Fritillary (*Melitaea athalia*) in the north Essex woods, 'bordering the road from Colchester to Ipswich.'[154] In his day the woods were some 700 acres in extent and were wonderful hunting grounds for insects. Here, it is said, abounded *athalia* until about 1890, when they were exterminated, and failed to establish themselves elsewhere in the county.

'SOME PEOPLE APPEAR TO HAVE MORE MONEY THAN WITS'

Doubleday's patent honesty naturally drew some forthright remarks from him from time to time, and he was ever jealous of the reputation of entomologists in this country. He was never slow in speaking plainly when he felt the necessity; the labelling, whether through carelessness or design, of foreign specimens as British never failed to arouse his scorn, and the gullibility of collectors made him raise his hands in horror. As an example, he contributed a long letter to the *Zoologist* of 1856 about the authenticity of certain specimens of the scarce Queen of Spain Fritillary and Bath White butterflies which E. C. Buxton of Warrington announced had been captured in this country; Buxton referred particularly to some unset Queen of Spain Fritillaries for which he paid 2s. 0d. each from a Mr. Seaman, who was a collector and dealer of Ipswich, and who said he had taken the insects himself. Of these rarities Doubleday soon disposed:—

'These specimens were no doubt part of a lot, which I know he had in this state from the late John Hoy Esq. of Higham, who took them on the Continent. Mr. Seaman would not have sold British specimens of this insect at 2s. 0d. each. When at his house he showed me rows of *L. chryseis* (Purple-edged Copper) and *L. virgaureae* (Scarce Copper), all of which he assured me were taken by himself in Britain: I purchased three or four specimens for examination, and upon relaxing them the wings returned to the position in which they had originally been set upon the Continent.'

Doubleday went on to develop the argument against accepting without verification specimens as British: 'As another proof of the care required before admitting species to be British, I may mention that three specimens of *Phigalia*[155] were sent to me to name, with a statement that they were "unquestionably British" and with two, localities were sent. The moment I saw them I recognised them as specimens taken by a collector in the United States a few years previously, and upon their being shown to him, he at once said that I was correct. I knew the insect perfectly well as a N. American species, and from the pin and the way in which they were set, I knew who collected them.'

The above extract shows that in spite of Doubleday's retiring disposition, he kept abreast of events in the entomological world, and his astuteness quickly earned the respect of the dealers who were only too willing to take advantage of unbusinesslike amateur collectors. Doubleday also wrote to Buxton privately about these reputed British specimens, no doubt giving him further warnings; he felt very strongly about the undesirability of introducing Continental specimens into this country, and nearly 20 years later he reiterated his belief that most rare specimens, professedly British, are Continental which could be bought there for as little as 3d or 6d each, pointing out that so long as collectors were willing to pay as many pounds as they cost in pence for a specimen, he could see no likelihood of a stop being made to these disreputable proceedings.

He emphasized that it was almost impossible to identify British specimens, as living pupae were obtained regularly in France and Germany and sent here, and further, living butterflies and moths could be easily obtained by post from the Continent. When these Continental species are introduced, Doubleday rightly pointed out that all interest in making a British collection is destroyed.[156] Looked at in rather a wider view, entomologists could easily be seriously misled when studying the geographical range and ecology of species, if foreign specimens were incorrectly labelled as British.

About this time he had occasion to write to a friend, Thomas Cooke, and in his letter he took the opportunity of mentioning this matter. The letter is an interesting one and is therefore reproduced in full below:—

My dear Sir,

It is a long time since anything has passed between us. I quite thought I should have seen you and your daughter on Sunday when the strawberries were ripe. I had bushels and gathered them every day for six weeks. The show of the Essex and Herts. Horticultural Society was held here in the grounds of John Henry Smee on the 15th of July and I was awarded the first prize for strawberries. Some of those in the dish which I sent weighed 3½ oz. each, and they were all gathered from runners planted in August last year.

Two or three years ago you asked me to get you a pair of Missel Thrushes, which I did—there is a service tree in the field between forty and fifty yards from the garden and for the last week dozens of these thrushes have come after the berries—an invalid friend of mine is fond of these small birds when nicely cooked as she cannot take much food and yesterday I shot ten Missel thrushes, nine of which I sent to her. The other is such a very beautiful bird that I will send it to you in the morning—it is one of the finest specimens I ever saw—neither of the others were at all like it.

The moths seem to have disappeared here—I have not seen a single *Agrotis segetum* or *exclamationis* and some years dozens of them would fly out of the beds when I was gathering strawberries.

I am strongly of opinion that some of the Canterbury dealers are introducing a lot of continental specimens as British. I believe nine-tenths of the rare British *lepidoptera* in the recent collections are Continental. I have a great many sent to me to examine and there was not one British specimen among them. Some people appear to have more money than wits and will give five pounds at King Street for what they could buy for fivepence.

Two weeks ago I spent a couple of days with my old and valued friend, Wm. C. Hewitson. What a splendid collection of butterflies he now has—he said you and your daughter were there on the 15th June and he appeared to be annoyed that through some inadvertence you were not asked in for lunch—he said I should tell you that it was unintentional.

The afternoon Sunday train is discontinued for the winter.

With kind regards I am
My dear Sir,
Yours very sincerely,
HENRY DOUBLEDAY.

Mr. Tho. Cooke.

The introduction of foreign specimens was undoubtedly a subject which concerned him greatly throughout his life. Many years earlier (in 1847) he had also contributed a long letter to the *Zoologist*, the heading of which read 'Remarks on the Introduction of Exotic Insects into Collections professedly British', in which he expressed the view that entomologists had now more desire to examine for themselves than to follow blindly their predecessors, but that many insects labelled 'British' in collections were undoubtedly foreign, and in support of this cited several examples. He then proceeded to list a number of species which in various collections were labelled as British, quite wrongly, Doubleday insisted, and gave the localities abroad where they occur. He concluded the letter as follows:—'I now take leave of the subject, hoping one day to see a catalogue of British insects a little more correct than any yet published.' In fact it was in that year that Doubleday himself first published his *Catalogue*.

Again and again Doubleday returned to the attack, insisting that the greater part of the interest in collections would go, if foreign specimens were introduced. C. R. Bree wrote[157] to the *Zoologist* in 1857, asking that foreign specimens should be obtained to complete British collections to which of course Doubleday strongly disagreed, stating that in the previous year a dealer who constantly advertised rarities, had sold hundreds of specimens obtained from the Continent, set in British style. He also pointed out that most British species could be obtained for threepence or sixpence abroad.

The activities of these unscrupulous dealers were exposed by P. B. M. Allan in his delightful book *Talking of Moths* (1943), in which his account of these 'Kentish buccaneers', as he picturesquely termed them, makes fascinating reading; several of the more notorious living, as Allan signified, in that county.

Doubleday on several occasions drew attention to the sudden abundance and then disappearance of that very well known butterfly, the Small Tortoiseshell.[158] The Camberwell Beauty is another member of the same family, but very rare in this country, and the capture near Epping of this beautiful insect, the dream of all young entomologists, was recorded by Doubleday on the 12th September 1846; it was a female and another of the same species was also seen.[159] Many years later in 1872 he was discussing in the *Entomologist's Monthly Magazine* the question of the migration of this magnificent insect, referring to that year as its *'annus mirabilis* in England'. He gave to Newman a long description of its larva, from a Continental specimen, which Newman published in the *Entomologist* in 1870.

The Purple Emperor butterfly, although never so exceedingly rare as the Camberwell Beauty, is uncommon enough, but the Forest always contained a few specimens. Doubleday's examples were bred from larvae, and he gave this clue to their discovery:—'I have found the young larvae of *iris* in March on the catkins of the sallow shaken from the trees in Ongar Park Woods.'[160]

Some discussion took place in the pages of the *Entomologist* in 1866 on the subject of the times of emergence of the sexes of various insects. The matter was first raised by the Rev. J. Greene who doubted the theory that the males were the first to emerge. Doubleday was quite definite that they were, as a general rule, and said he had repeatedly proved Lewin correct in his work on *British Butterflies* (1795) when he wrote of The Brown Hairstreak (*Thecla betulae*) 'the male butterfly appears on the wing about the middle of August; the female is nearly 14 days later before it emerges from the chrysalis.' Doubleday also supported his argument by his observation of a number of common species, such as *janira* ((*jurtina*)—Meadow Brown) and *tithonus* (Hedge Brown) in which the females always emerge a week or ten days after the males. In the wall of his Epping garden hundreds of *Anthophora acervorum* used to breed and on no occasion did he see a female until the males had been out for several days, thus indicating that he thought the prior appearance of males was not confined to lepidoptera. With regard to the Dragonflies he is equally emphatic that the males appear first, stating that the females are not attractive to the males after a few days. He also bred a large number of the moth *Hadena thalassina* (Pale-shouldered

Brocade) from the eggs of a single female, the breeding cage for the larvae being kept in a room close to a window facing north and the room unheated. The first ten or eleven moths to emerge were all males; in spite of this experience, however, he was inclined to think 'that the evidence afforded on this question by insects in captivity is of little or no value.'

NATURAL SELECTION

Today we are well advanced in our knowledge of the meaning and character of melanism in lepidoptera, but in Doubleday's time a melanic specimen was looked upon as an unusual variety and the scientific reason for its occurrence not understood. Although many English moths are becoming darker, one, the Peppered Moth, is considered to be the first example of a Geometer which could strike off in a black form without a gradual change:[161] this melanic moth first occurred about the middle of the 19th Century in the manufacturing areas of the north of England, Manchester, it is said, being the scene of its first capture in 1848. Spreading south, it reached London a few years before the turn of the century and is now commoner than the type over most of England.

This kind of melanism, known as industrial melanism, is attributable to natural selection, and in the case of the Peppered Moth this selection has been instrumental in directing the evolution from the existing pre-industrial revolution type to the melanic.[162] One hundred years ago the dark variety formed less than 1% of the population in polluted industrial areas, and now it is at least 99%, and throughout eastern England it is never less than 80%. The melanic form is controlled by a single dominant Mendelian gene, rather more vigorous than the type, but this would not have survived and flourished if the form had not been 'pre-adapted' to favourable conditions which were only subsequently realised, i.e. the industrial revolution, and consequent pollution of the air by smoke, and the killing of lichen on the tree-trunks. Natural selection, of which this insect is an obvious example, was first brought before the public a hundred years ago by Darwin and Wallace.

This black form was known for a long time as *f. doubledayaria* Millière, but is now superseded by its synonym *f. carbonaria* Jordan.

The colours of larvae, as well as those of the imagines play an important, yet not always obvious, part in the working of natural selection, and in recent years a great deal of experimental work has been undertaken. Doubleday sent a note[163] on the colours of larvae to the *Entomologist's Monthly Magazine* without committing himself, however, to the acceptance or otherwise of Darwin's theories; his contribution was entitled *Note on the Relations between Colour and Edibility in Larvae*, and read as follows:—

'It has often been said that birds do not feed upon larvae which are gaily coloured. A dozen years since, I planted a quantity of Hounds-tongue in the garden, and placed larvae of *Callimorpha dominula* (Scarlet Tiger) upon it, and the species completely established itself here. This spring there were hundreds of caterpillars; but about three weeks since, I noticed that their numbers were decreasing, and could not account for it. At last I found that a pair of large tits (*Parus major*), which had a nest in a hole in a tree just outside the garden, fetched them away to feed their young ones. Now this is one of the brightest-coloured larvae that I know of. The larvae of the *Zygaenae* (the Burnets) are also gaily-coloured, and they are the favourite food of cuckoos.'

The intensive study of sexual behaviour and differences in numerous species of plant and animal life, and hybridisation, formed the basis of Darwin's evolutionary theories. How much Doubleday contributed to these is problematical, but possibly not very much, as Doubleday although a penetrating observer had no great scientific endowment; but there is no doubt that the two naturalists did assist each other in the correspondence which passed between them, and occasionally Darwin made reference to Doubleday in his scientific works. Edward Doubleday's observations were also valued, an example being in the *Descent of Man* in which Darwin quotes him in connection with neuration of the wings of butterflies differing between the sexes.[164]

Edward gave a description before the Entomological Society in London on 3rd March 1845 of a butterfly taken by Darwin in Brazil in 1832 which was curious in that it made an unusual clicking noise when flying—there was 'a peculiar structure in the wings of this butterfly, which seems to be the means of its making this noise . . .' Doubleday said of this insect, *Papilio (Ageronia) feronia*: 'it is remarkable for having a sort of drum at the base of the fore-wings, between the costal nervure and the sub-costal. These two nervures, moreover, have a peculiar screw like a diaphragm or vessel in the interior.'[165]

The study of the proportion of the numbers of the sexes of insects was a part of Darwin's necessary investigation when forming his theories on selection, and this subject was discussed before the Entomological Society in 1868, a number of entomologists, including Stainton, taking the view that the females were more numerous.[166] Doubleday and some other naturalists took the opposite view, 'and are convinced' said Darwin 'that they have reared from the egg and caterpillar states a larger proportion of males than of females.' In support of his views Doubleday took the opportunity of drawing Darwin's attention to the Sale Catalogue of the famous professional Continental lepidopterist, Dr. Staudinger. In this list (*Lepidopteren— Doubblettren Liste*, Berlin No. X, 1866) some 300 species of butterflies were offered for sale, and of the rarer ones all the males were cheaper than the females, with the exception of only one species. Of the 2,000 species of moths in the Catalogue, the females of only eleven species were more expensive than the males. For Doubleday this provided evidence that the difference could be accounted for only by the numbers of males exceeding the females, at any rate, so far as butterflies were concerned, 'and' says Darwin, 'no man in England has had more experience.' Darwin took the same view as Doubleday, Staudinger himself however not subscribing to this conclusion, attributing it to other reasons.

It is interesting to note that Doubleday's friend, H. W. Bates, when writing of his travels in his famous book, *The Naturalist on the Amazons*, mentions that he found male butterflies much more numerous than females.

The subject of the attraction of the sexes was not one to which Doubleday appears to have devoted much time, but he made a few observations to Darwin which the latter recorded. As an example of 'assembling' he mentioned to Darwin that in one day when virgin females of the moths *Lasiocampa quercus* (Oak Eggar) and *Saturnia carpini* ((*S. pavonia*)—Emperor) were kept under confinement, some 50 to 100 males of both species were attracted to the females. Another observation by Doubleday was also quoted by Darwin in *The Descent of Man*, in connection with the death-tick (*Anobium tessellatum*). He had closely watched a female twice or thrice ticking, and found her in the course of an hour or so united with a male, and on one occasion surrounded by several males. Of this sex-call he told Darwin 'the noise is produced by the insect raising itself on its legs as high as it can, and then striking its thorax five or six times, in rapid succession, against the substance upon which it is sitting.'

In the same book too, when discussing the attraction of colour in flowers for butterflies and moths, Darwin says: 'The common white butterfly, as I hear from Mr. Doubleday, often flies down to a bit of paper on the ground, no doubt mistaking it for one of its own species.'

The question of the length of time which certain butterflies and moths spend in the pupal stage has frequently puzzled entomologists, the period often varying considerably. The pupa, for example, of the Oak Eggar remains, as Doubleday pointed out in the *Entomologist* in 1873, usually one month in this stage: but, he said, occasionally a year is thus spent. Some species remain two or three years—it was in the autumn of 1873 that he wrote 'A person residing here has now some living pupae of *Cucullia verbasci* (the Mullein Moth) from larvae obtained in 1869.'[167] On the same subject, he mentioned in a letter to the same journal about a year later (October 1874) that in September 1872 his friend F. O. Standish, had sent him some larvae of *Emmelesia unifasciata* (Haworth's Carpet) which he reared and about a dozen moths appeared in August 1873. Just a year later three of four more emerged; and on 12th October 1874 in the letter to the *Entomologist* he wrote 'A few days since I examined all the cocoons, and found 37 living pupae.' Doubleday himself had taken this very rare moth some years before at Epping.[168] The length of time many species remain in this state accounted largely, said Doubleday, for their abundance in some years and scarcity in others.

'SUGARING'

The well known method of capturing moths at night on patches of 'sugar' was first used by Doubleday, and by this means our collections have been greatly enriched. After the death of the Doubleday brothers and of Henry's capable assistant, English, some controversy arose as to whether James English or Henry Doubleday was actually the first to employ this means of collecting, although it does seem abundantly clear now that Doubleday must be given the credit for it.[169]

The confusion arose after a talk by English to the Essex Field Club in 1881[170]—six years after Doubleday's death—entitled *The first night's 'sugaring' in England—A reminiscence of Epping Forest in 1843.* Although he stated at the commencement of the lecture that he claimed no merit as discoverer, English mentioned that it was certainly himself, 'who', in his own words, 'first applied "sugar", practically as a valuable adjunct to net and lanthorn.' He had noticed, he said, together with Doubleday, that empty sugar hogsheads placed outside their warehouse at the shop premises in Epping attracted moths, particularly in the autumn and rainy seasons. Also he noted that in one fine day during the summer the bees would clear off all the adhering sugar. English went on to say that apart from the hogsheads, Doubleday never utilised this knowledge for the capture of insects. Having observed moths on a plum tree in the garden, attracted by 'honeydew' on the leaves, he said he then had the idea of producing artificial 'honeydew' to sprinkle on the foliage of trees and bushes, and this, English said, worked extremely well. 'I wish my brother home to help me set your captures, you bring so many good things' was the remark Edward Doubleday was supposed to have made to English, who in his lecture gave his experiences of 'sugaring' during the summer of 1843, which was a particularly good year for *noctuae*. Henry was in Paris at that time and upon his return he was very surprised, and after sending for him to learn the details and a few experiments Doubleday wrote to Newman to tell him all about it. So related English, who was apparently quite certain of the year—1843, when Doubleday was in Paris—although the lecture was given nearly 40 years later. English died in January 1888, having been ill for several months, and it was in that year when Miller Christy, in a letter to the Essex Field Club, and printed in the *Essex Naturalist*, made a thorough investigation into English's claim.

Although the Essex Field Club was established in 1880, and its *Transactions and Proceedings* were published from that date, it was not until 1887 that the *Essex Naturalist*, the Journal of the Club, first appeared. It will be seen from Miller Christy's letter, given below, that it was well *before* his journey to France that Doubleday was using this method of catching moths. This is what Miller Christy said:—

. . . 'I cannot avoid the conclusion that the memory of the late Mr. English was somewhat at fault when he made these statements. I have now before me one hundred and one interesting letters written by Henry Doubleday between 30.8.31 and March 2nd 1846 to the late T. C. Heysham of Carlisle, and kindly lent to me by the representatives of the latter gentleman. In one of these letters dated 11.8.41, I read as follows:—

"Since I last wrote, the weather has been much the same as for some time past. Last night and this morning it rained very fast, and about ¾" of rain fell. It is also very windy. So many wet evenings are a hindrance to my captures of *lepidoptera*, but I go out every night that is at all tolerable. By taking some sugar and water and brushing it on the trunks of trees, or sprinkling it on the bushes, you attract an immense number of moths, and about an hour after sunset they remain quite quiet, and with a light you may select what you want. Last night, although raining, I saw scores of Noctuae." . . .

From this it appears that, not only had the idea of sugaring occurred to Henry Doubleday, but that he had also actually put it into practice with considerable success *at least two years* before the date at which Mr. English tells us he himself originated the method. Moreover, I cannot find in the letters written in 1843 any mention of 'sugaring', except one, which shows that as early as March 17th, Henry Doubleday was practising this method of taking insects much as a matter of course, for he writes:—

"Just after I had sent my letter to you on Friday night, I went down our field to look after moths on the sugar, and was surprised to see the tail of a comet of immense length."

This was *before* his visit to Paris, where he went on July 21st, returning to Epping on the evening of August 2nd, having then been away only a few days.

Further than this, however, I find in the *Entomologist* for October 1842 (Vol. 1 p. 407) a note of Henry Doubleday's, stating that in the previous August he had taken two specimens of *Polia occulta*,[171] "both sucking sugar which I had placed on the trunks of some trees to attract moths"; while in the *Zoologist* for the following year (Vol. 1 p. 201) appeared a communication from Henry Doubleday entitled "Note on the Capture of *Noctuae* with Sugar in the Autumn of 1842 at Epping". This note is dated 31.5.43—nearly 2 months before he went to Paris. I think, therefore, that the late Mr. English must be unhesitatingly pronounced in error; and although the error is not of great scientific importance, still I think it is well to have it corrected. It merely transfers the honour of having originated this now-well-known method of taking insects from one prominent Essex naturalist to another. In connection with this subject, the following note by Edward Doubleday will be of interest. It appeared in the *Entomological Magazine* (Vol. 1 p. 310) and is dated "Epping, Nov. 21st, 1832:— *Singular Mode of Capturing Noctuae*—I would recommend to your readers a plan by which I have captured many good *lepidoptera*, as will be seen by the list I send herewith (69 species named). It is simply to lay a sugar hogshead which has just been emptied (and to which, of course, a small quantity of sugar will adhere) in an open space near a garden or field. In the course of a night or two, it will be visited by numbers of *Noctuae*, amongst which will not infrequently be found some of the rarer species. The *Noctuae* continue to visit it, particularly on moist evenings, as long as it retains any saccharine matter." '

The Editor of the *Essex Naturalist*, William Cole, was not, however, in entire agreement with Miller Christy's conclusions, and his note in reply was as follows:—

'Mr. Christy has certainly pointed out a serious discrepancy in the two statements, and the lamented death of Mr. English renders it now impossible to clear up the difficulty. We feel sure, however, that the error was merely one of date. Mr. English wrote from memory; and supposing that his first experiments in the use of 'sugar' were made during one of Mr. Doubleday's absences from Epping, it is perfectly easy to see how the blunder might have arisen. Knowing that Mr. Doubleday was away at the time, imperfect recollection may have connected that absence with the historical visit to Paris, and the period of the latter event being known, an erroneous date was thereby assigned to *"The 1st Night's Sugaring in England".*'

Despite this opinion, it is now accepted by most entomologists that English must have been mistaken, and that Doubleday was in fact the first employer of this method. English, said Cole, might have mistaken another of Doubleday's absences for his journey to Paris; but it was extremely rare for him to be away from home for any length of time, for he was no traveller, and in fact it is recorded that between the years 1846 and 1873 he spent only two nights away from his own house.[172] As Miller Christy said, the point is unimportant, but it would have been more satisfactory if the matter could have been definitely decided at the time, but alas! before the time of Miller Christy's letter the Doubledays, English, and their friend Newman had all passed on, leaving no further evidence.[173]

Doubleday explained his method of 'sugaring', as stated above in the letter quoted by Miller Christy to Heysham but one well-known author writing on Essex worthies has erroneously concluded that he 'sugared' the trees in the morning before opening his shop, and then after closing at night would collect the trapped moths. The 'sugar', of course, was not put on to catch the insects, but in the evening to attract them by its sweetness, and they could be caught whilst sucking the rich mixture; in fact many moths seem to dislike actually alighting on the patch, but prefer to feast from the margin.

For over 130 years, therefore, 'sugaring' has now been used extensively by entomologists as one of the principal methods of moth collection. During his lifetime Doubleday made reference from time to time of captures at sugar, and indeed, from 1842 onwards he kept his friends and the scientific journals advised, when he thought it necessary, of unusual specimens captured in this manner; yet many collectors were unaware of the best methods to adopt, and in 1875 a correspondent to the *Entomologist*, Charles Clifton, asked for advice as to the best time for 'sugaring', to which the Editor, Newman, replied himself, stating that no specific time was necessary and that it was usual to sugar the trees, and make a succession of rounds at about half-hourly intervals, starting at dusk. But Newman, who was then well over 70, had not a great deal of experience, 'not liking night-work', as he explained.

The Rev. Thomas Crallan also answered giving details of his nocturnal adventures, and Doubleday responded with the advice to put the sugar warm on the trees shortly before sunset, and the collector will find the greatest number of visitors about three-quarters of an hour after sunset. He went on to warn the correspondent that it would be useless to use sugar near lime trees when they are in blossom, and also when 'honeydew' is abundant. Of his own experience he said, 'There is a row of 17 lime trees in the field adjoining my garden, and I have sugared the trunks for more than 30 years in every month, except the four winter ones—November, December, January, February. Upon these trees I have captured nearly every *Noctua* which occurs in this neighbourhood.'[174] He was an active man fond of out-door exercise, who it is said, used in summer to rise with the sun, which led him to observe that many species of moths also visited 'sugar' in the very early morning. The Epping Quaker's letter[175] was written towards the end of his life, for within two months he was dead.

It is also worth recording that nearly two years before his trip to Paris, in the preface dated October 1841, of *British Moths and their Transformations* (Humphreys and Westwood) reference was made to the use by Doubleday of a method of attracting moths by applying a mixture of sugar and water to trees, an operation which was reported to be very successful. J. O. Westwood was responsible for the characters and descriptions of the moths in this book which contained many beautifully coloured plates by H. Noel Humphreys, and numerous references to Doubleday.

English had mentioned in his lecture that he observed the honey-dew on the plum trees, and letters from entomologists occasionally appeared in scientific journals on this subject. Doubleday gave his views on the connection between aphides and honeydew in a letter to the *Entomologist* in 1873, quoting the Abbé Boissier de Sauvages of nearly a century earlier. He also described how a number of currant bushes which were growing against a wall in his Epping garden, facing north-west, were quite healthy in the May of 1868, but became suddenly heavily covered with honeydew, and after becoming slowly weaker, most of them died in the following winter.

One of the earliest recorded contributions made to Entomology by Doubleday was printed in the *Entomologist* in its first volume of 1841; in it he described his success in capturing moths, chiefly *Noctuae*, at night as they fed at the blossoms of sallows. This spring-time activity of Doubleday's was at that time a novel procedure, but it has been followed since by countless collectors with great success.

OBSERVATIONS ON SOME OTHER WILD LIFE IN ESSEX

Some attention was paid to the dragonflies of the Epping district, which was particularly rich in these insects due to the numerous secluded ponds occurring in the Forest and it was in 1841 that he contributed to the *Entomologist* a short note on a genus of dragon-flies, *Sympetrum*. Thirty years later, when Doubleday gave his total local list to the *Entomologist's Monthly Magazine*, in September 1871, it contained no less than 30 species, about two-thirds of the total of known British ones, and in addition the name of another species which was seen and identified but not captured. This is what he wrote in the preface to the synopsis:—'Having captured a large portion of our British *Libellulae* in the neighbourhood of Epping, I thought a list of them might be interesting to some of your readers.

I regret to say that some of the best localities are destroyed, and I am not certain that all the species enumerated are now to be found here. The nomenclature is that adopted by Mr. McLachlan, in his valuable catalogue of *British Neuroptera.*'

There could surely be few places in Britain which could produce such a number of species; for example a correspondent to this magazine, J. E. Fletcher, reported finding but one-third of the British species in the Worcester district, up to the same year, i.e. 1871.

These records of Doubleday's were quoted extensively in W. J. Lucas' book *British Dragonflies* (1900), and in the *Naturalists' Gazette* (1890) the Editor in his article on *British Dragonflies* gave Epping as the locality of many species—clearly Doubleday's records, although he is not mentioned by name. Pinniger, however, made numerous references to them when writing on the *Dragonflies of Epping Forest* in 1932 and he specified 22 Forest dragonflies recording a number which were given by Doubleday in his list, but not noticed in later lists: Doubleday's fears that some species had disappeared were therefore justified, and it appears that at least eight species ceased to occur there within sixty years. W. Harwood, in the list of Essex Dragonflies in the *Victoria County History* (1903) gives Doubleday as the authority for the record of many rare species captured at Epping.

Although primarily a lepidopterist, all wild life, particularly of his local Epping area, came within the sphere of his life-long interest, but spiders and some insect families appeared to receive little attention from him. However, he reported in the *Zoologist* the finding of a locust in an Epping field in 1846 (this was probably a Migratory Locust, which occasionally reaches this country), and a few of his notes on the other forms of life may be of interest.

Of the half-dozen species of batrachians inhabiting these Islands, all can be found in Essex,[176] but it was surely only his enthusiasm as a naturalist, not as a gourmet, which made him responsible for the attempt to naturalize the Edible Frog (*Rana esculenta*) in nearby Epping Forest ponds. It is very doubtful whether any of these introduced colonies now survive, although they apparently flourished for a time.

Edward Newman described a visit to a colony, in a paragraph in the *Zoologist* in 1848, as follows:—

'Mr. Henry Doubleday having received from Foulmire (Fowl-

72

mere) Fen some living specimens of this truly beautiful frog, turned them loose near a pond not far from his residence. They soon migrated to another pond, and there have made themselves perfectly at home. Mr. Doubleday has never seen them on land, but they may often be observed seated on the floating pond weed, watching the *agrions* and other insects which fly over the water, and occasionally leaping to catch them when within reach. A few days since I had the pleasure of watching these frogs, and would gladly have captured one to bring home, but he dived so nimbly as to elude the net. Mr. Doubleday describes their croaking in Spring as being very loud and remarkable: at this season they would sometimes sit on a rail which overhung the water, and exercise their vocal powers in great style.'

The colony of Edible Frogs at Foulmire had been in existence for many years, and it was here that this frog was first noted in England by the zoologist Thomas Bell; Bell, who was born in 1792, said his father, the surgeon, also named Thomas, described to him the noise which the frogs made at Whaddon and Foulmire. Doubleday must have collected his specimens shortly before Foulmire Fen was drained in 1847, because when that happened the colony came to an end.[177] About the year 1844, two specimens of this frog from Foulmire were given by F. Bond, and two by Yarrell, to the British Museum, and they have proved to be of the variety *lessonae*, which is the short-legged South European form of *esculenta*.

It is not known how long Doubleday's introductions to the Epping Forest ponds lasted, but it is interesting to note that almost exactly 100 years later enthusiastic amateurs attempted a reintroduction to these ponds, and it is stated that in 1948 a colony, estimated to be about four years old, was seen in Whipps Cross Pond, in the south end of the Forest.

Apart from this episode, Doubleday does not seem to have commented much on the other frogs or reptiles which occurred locally, probably feeling that little new to scientific knowledge could be added, but certainly the Forest abounded in snakes and lizards. Toads he mentioned only incidentally when talking to Newman about his 'sugaring' expeditions, when he said they frequently waited under the sugar for the moths which would occasionally drop from the sugar patch to the ground. These recollections were made by Newman when a correspondent to the *Entomologist* in 1875 recounted a similar experience, and some fifteen years earlier such occurrences were also mentioned in the *Zoologist*.

Of bats Doubleday gave his Epping Forest list to the *Zoologist* in a letter dated Dec. 1841. His catalogue did not, however, include the Serotine Bat, a specimen of which was shot at Pattiswick Hall[178] near Coggeshall in 1881, but of the more common ones, he once told Edward Newman that he took a Natterer's Bat in his insect net when mothing, and he found on one occasion more than 100 in an old garret.[179]

Numerous bats frequented the grotto of Stanford Rivers Hall, the home of Doubleday's friend, Robert Dix. In the *Zoologist*[180] Doubleday described at some length this interesting building, mentioning also the finding of numerous wings of moths which were contained in the grotto; he was certain these wings were dropped by bats when devouring moths on the wing, and this view was shared by Newman, but not by all naturalists. One well known entomologist, Stephen Clogg, had occasion to write to the *Zoologist*[181] a few years later (1869) to record the finding of the wing of a rare moth in a spider's web, and he felt very strongly that the presence of detached wings found in places such as this grotto was primarily due to spiders. Clogg said he believed no two men were never more mistaken in the matter than Doubleday and Newman, although he felt himself, as he put it, 'a minnow attacking tritons', when opposing their views.

Turning to the larger fauna of the Forest, it is of interest to note that Doubleday purchased what was probably the last Marten to be caught and killed in that area. This was trapped in April 1853 by Mr. Luffman, head keeper to the Lord of the Manor of Loughton, Mr. Maitland. It was found in a covert near Loughton, a few miles from the town of Epping, and was kept a few days by Luffman before he took it to Epping where Doubleday bought it.[182] Several times since then reports have been received of martens seen in the locality—one from James English who saw one near Ambresbury Banks in the Forest, on 30th July 1883, but it is extremely unlikely that it will ever be observed there again, owing to the increasing urbanisation of the whole area.

Notes on the Mammalia of Norfolk by Mr. Gunn were contributed to the *Zoologist* in 1870, and in the article Gunn recounted a tale, told him by a gamekeeper, of a hedgehog springing on to and attacking a trapped rabbit. Doubleday was extremely critical of this story, and insisted that it could not possibly be true, and in this he was strongly supported by Newman; hedgehogs are, of course, favourite subjects of rural superstition, yet perhaps the game-keeper's account of the incident contained a germ of truth, for it is now authenticated that hedgehogs will attack and devour very young rabbits, hunting them out in their burrows;[183] but the gamekeeper gave no details of the one which was trapped.

ILLNESS

The final decade of the life of Henry Doubleday, the last of his family at Epping, was lived almost in seclusion, pursued by ill-health from which he rarely seemed free; a perusal of such of his letters which survive, reveals that only too frequently was he labouring under severe physical handicaps during this period: indeed, long before then, in 1856, he disclosed that he was depressed and unwell. A letter to his 'dear friend' Thomas Dix, who farmed Stanford Rivers Hall near Romford for many years, strikes a rather pathetic note: Doubleday had been in touch with George Loddiges[184] of Hackney in 1842 and 1843 on methods of stuffing birds, and he now discussed the same subject with Dix some twelve or thirteen years later, enclosing in one letter a missive from Loddiges on the same subject, obviously feeling it would be of value to Dix. Doubleday told Dix that he did not want Loddiges' letter returned, stating 'my bird stuffing days are over'. Although undated, it was probably written within a short time of another he wrote to Dix dated 31st January 1856, in which he referred to the death of his relative John Double-day of the British Museum. This time he enclosed with the letter a London sale catalogue, and referred to his difficulty in writing because his hand was no better, also mentioning that at Epping 'it is dull here', and he seemed to have nothing to write about. Clearly he was feeling depressed and although it was the end of January, it was quite unlike him not to take a keen interest in the wildlife of the countryside and to find plenty to occupy both his mind and his pen. But he commented that he had seen Willow-grouse and Ptarmigan from Norway on a recent visit to London, bringing some back for James English, but whether for the table or stuffing is not clear!

About two years later[185] when again writing to Dix, he sent at the same time a number of rare birds, stuffed but not in cases, including a White-winged Crossbill, White Wagtail, Savi's Warbler (this was the one shot by Mr. Bond near Cambridge, mentioned by

Yarrell in his *British Birds*), Bridled Guillemot, King Eider ('from the Scotch Isles') and in addition a few foreign birds: he explained that there was no more probability of his doing any more work in ornithology, as his state of health was precarious.

Not only did Doubleday suffer from indifferent health, but financial worry seemed at times almost too much for him; it is possible that neglect of his grocery business in the High Street at Epping may have contributed to this, but it is an unfortunate fact that since 1866 when a bank which held a substantial amount of his money collapsed,[186] he fought a losing battle against bankruptcy. The thought of being deprived of his collections and his library, upon which he had devoted such time, enthusiasm and care, and of leaving his house, was a continual nightmare to him, affecting him both mentally and physically, and it is incredible that during this worrying time he continued to pursue his studies when he was well enough to write.

In the archives of the British Museum (Natural History) there are ten letters written by Doubleday to the Hon. Thomas de Grey (later Lord Walsingham), covering the period from 6th February 1867 to 27th October 1870, which were probably acquired when the vast Walsingham collection of insects and library were presented to them in 1910.[187] Most of these letters refer to moths sent to Doubleday for identification, and throw little fresh light on Doubleday's life and character, and it is clear that a considerable interchange of insects took place. The following extract is from a letter to Grey dated 1st February 1868:—

'Your very liberal present of game arrived this morning and I return you my sincerest thanks for your great kindness—it is indeed a most acceptable present and if all is well this year I hope to be able to make you some little return for your kindness—I also thank you for returning the box, but I did not wish you to give yourself any trouble about it.'—

a gift, which, bearing in mind Doubleday's financial straits, must have been very welcome. In this letter Doubleday referred also to a large *noctua* he had been asked to identify, taken by Mr. Harding at Deal in 1867; apparently he had discussed the insect with Grey but they were both perplexed about it, Doubleday commenting 'a few weeks since a Russian Entomologist—Baron von Nolcken, was here and he says it is probably an exotic species accidentally imported' . . . It was finally identified as a variety of *Xylophasia*

zollikoferi by Dr. Staudinger, to whom Doubleday had sent it.[188]
An extract from a further letter about six months later contains not quite so cheerful a note, alluding to his recent ill-health:—
To The Hon. Thomas de Grey
Merton Hall
Thetford   19 August 1868
Honble and dear Sir,
    Just before your letter arrived I sent a box to the Railway Station enclosing your *Eupaecilia* and a few *geometrae* for your acceptance—I ought to have returned your moth long ago and must ask you to excuse my neglect—I have not been in good health for some time past and have suffered from almost constant headache for the last two months, but I am much better now . . .'
The distressing headaches were not mentioned in a letter to Grey a month later, in which he acknowledged the gift of some insects, as follows:—
Honble and Dear Sir,   15 September 1868
    The box which you so kindly sent only reached me this morning —it has been delayed somewhere—I will enclose the label and you will see that the Thetford post mark is Sept. 11th and the London one Sept. 14th and ours the 15th—the insects, however, are uninjured and I beg to return you my sincerest thanks for them— they are most beautiful specimens and very nicely set.
    I never before saw *Callixsparsata* so fine and I feel truly obliged to you for the series—it is a very rare species in France and I should like to send a pair to my very kind friend M. Guenée.'

THE RETREAT, YORK

Early in 1871 it became clear that Henry Doubleday could no longer continue in business: his health had finally broken down and his possessions would have to be sold to satisfy his creditors. The tiny Quaker Meeting at Epping, with its half-a-dozen members was unable to give him the substantial financial support required to prevent his property being sold, although it is known that individual Friends helped him in this way. The immediate action which was required, however, was to arrange for medical treatment, and the responsibility for this was accepted by the Quaker Monthly Meeting, of which the Epping Meeting was a part; a place was quickly found for him in the Retreat, the independent Quaker Mental Hospital at

York, and there he spent the first few months of 1871. At this Hospital there was no fixed scale of fees, patients paying what they could afford, so that the figures given in the Minute quoted below[189] were probably low, and incredibly so by present day standards:—

Minute 11. 'This Meeting is informed by the Overseers that it has been found necessary to place Henry Doubleday of Epping at the Retreat at York and that his own circumstances render it needful that the expense should be borne by this Meeting. Accordingly bills for his expenses at the Retreat amounting to £4.11.2 and for his medical attendance £2.12.— have been brought in, which our Treasurer is requested to discharge'.

From the time of his admittance to the Retreat, he made good progress towards recovery, and in reply to an enquiry from Henry's relative, William Doubleday of Coggeshall, the Medical Superintendent, Dr. Kitching wrote soon after Henry Doubleday arrived there:—

The Retreat, York
Dec. 29th—70

Dear Friend,

I may inform thee in answer to thy letter that Hy. Doubleday bore his journey to York as well as could be expected from the feeble state of his health. He was a good deal exhausted and in a state of great nervous agitation, but has not grown worse since his arrival but has a little improved, and we succeed in administering nourishment rather better than at first. His condition of body and mind is a good deal shattered and will take a considerable time in building up again, if we are favoured to succeed in doing it. Although sadly troubled with delusions of ruin and disaster to himself and all connected with him, he is very kind and grateful for that which is done for him, and I hope to see him gradually mend.

Whatever the ultimate result as regards his mind may be, I can form no idea of the length of time he may require for his restoration.

I am with love,
Thy Friend
J. Kitching

Wm Doubleday

The care and attention given to Doubleday at the Retreat had the desired results, and after a few months he was able to return to his home at Epping, which he had been longing to do. He was able to keep in touch with many friends and relatives while he was away, and frequently these letters, written under much nervous strain and requiring great physical effort, make pathetic reading, for so long had his whole world revolved round his secluded life at Epping with only Ann Main, a devoted distant cousin who ministered to his frugal needs, as companion. 'I don't get a great deal of sleep, but I always dream about my home' he wrote; perhaps he was able to make good progress by losing himself again in entomological studies, for after some weeks in the Retreat, his letters to colleagues, Stainton in particular, were full of scientific comment. In his letter to Stainton of 6th March 1871 he accepted his offer to send him Staudinger's *Catalogue*, concluding 'I see the spring flowers are getting out here and of course they are forwarder in the South. I wish I was at Epping where for more than fifty years I have watched their appearance with pleasure.'

Stainton quickly replied to this, and in a letter of 9th March 1871 Doubleday confirmed the *Catalogue*'s safe arrival—'I am most truly obliged to you for your great kindness in so promptly sending Dr. Staudinger's *Catalogue* which arrived this morning. I have not, of course, had time to examine it very closely but I have seen enough to make me regret more than ever that the Doctor did not visit this country before it was printed—I must regret that he has adopted Mr. Darwin's notions about species . . .' The rest of this letter is taken up mainly by further criticism of the *Catalogue*, but concludes again on an unhappy note:—

'I feel my sad position more and more and the future appears very uncertain—I certainly hoped that I should have ended my days in my beloved home and without that and the society of my kind friends life will not be worth much.'

Many enquiries were made of Edward Newman, who was known to be in close touch with Doubleday, regarding his progress, and Newman, to keep readers of the *Entomologist* informed, inserted a paragraph in the May 1871 number to the effect that after four months away from home, because of illness, on medical advice he was to abstain from much exertion for a time: but he expressed the wish that Doubleday would soon be able to pursue his former studies—a wish that was granted, for up to the time of his death in 1875 he was just as helpful in assisting fellow entomologists, and his correspondence, both to individuals and to journals, was maintained.

One additional worry for Doubleday at this time was the fate of his friend Achille Guenée, who lived in Châteaudun, about 60 miles south-west of Paris; hostilities were raging between the Prussians and the French, and it was known that many libraries and collections were damaged in the second siege of Paris. He wrote to Stainton on 9th May 1871, after his return home to Epping from the Retreat:—

'I saw a letter from Thomas Whitwell one of the "Friends" who went to France to distribute the money etc. subscribed by the Society for the relief of the sufferers from the war and he said that the Prussians burnt 250 houses in Châteaudun and robbed the inhabitants of almost everything that was valuable. I hope Guenée did not sustain any serious loss.

My arm is so painful that I cannot write much more but I must not conclude this letter without expressing my heartfelt gratitude to my truly kind friends—and to you especially—for their liberality and their kind exertions on my behalf—nothing, as you know is finally settled but I shall be truly glad to spend the short remaining portion of my life in the house in which I was born—my health is very much shattered and I could not bear much excitement of any kind now.'

He must have been greatly relieved to learn in due course that Guenée's own library and collections entirely escaped Prussian destruction, although those of another local entomologist, M. Estienne were taken.[190]

FINANCIAL RESCUE

During his stay in the Retreat his many friends had been busy looking for ways in which Doubleday's creditors could be satisfied, and for putting him in a position in which he could continue to live in Epping and receive a small weekly allowance for his maintenance, and if possible prevent dispersion of his unique collections. It was quickly decided that a subscription list should be prepared, so that certain collections and books, which meant so much to Doubleday, could be purchased at the sale of his property, and promises of annual subscriptions should be received to put him in receipt of an annual allowance. This fund-raising scheme was arranged and managed by his old friend Edward Newman who decided that it should be administered by three Trustees, although he had collected funds for these purposes before the Trustees were actually appointed.

The two letters quoted below[191] are from Newman to Gibson, the Quaker banker and botanist of Saffron Walden:

York Grove, Peckham.

My dear Friend,

In the matter of Henry Doubleday's affairs, to the funds in aid of whom thou has so kindly contributed—I propose that the collections should be purchased in the names of three trustees, and *not in his own name* but they should ever become available in liquidation of future debts incurred by H.D. and for this trustee-ship I select the names of

Joseph Gurney Barclay
George Stacey Gibson
James Hack Tuke

The purchase will be made with the funds already so kindly raised and no trouble whatever will be imposed on the trustees beyond the *disposal* of collections in case of Henry Doubleday's death, and *that* will be very readily accomplished through S. Stevens who has taken a kind interest in all the proceedings of this sad case.

Henry Doubleday is so much improving that I look forward to receiving Dr. Kitching's permission for his removal from York before very long, but I wish to be prepared with the names of trustees before that event takes place and my object in writing is to ask permission to use thine.

I am very sincerely thy friend,
Edward Newman.

G. Stacey Gibson.

This letter is undated, but was probably written in early March 1871, as Doubleday was only in the Retreat for four months.

Newman wrote a further letter to Gibson dated 22nd March 1871 reading as follows:—

York Grove, Peckham.

22.III.1871.

My dear Friend,

I am truly obliged for thy kind letter: I have a short note from Gurney Barclay by the same post allowing his name to stand as a trustee in company with thine and James H. Tuke's; and I cannot very courteously ask him to allow me to substitute *my own name* for *either* even if I saw the propriety or advantage of such a step which I certainly do not.

G   81

I believe we none of us estimate ourselves exactly at our proper value. I fear I should vastly *overrate* myself and thus render myself ridiculous; and I am quite sure thou would *underrate* thyself and so place thyself in a false position. It is therefore better to accept the world's estimate and I am quite sure this little world of subscribers to this fund will be better satisfied with the names I have suggested than with mine.

Perhaps James Tuke will kindly undertake the task of writing such a note to Henry Doubleday as shall set his mind at ease with regard to making any use he pleases of the collections while at the same time conveying to him the fact that he is not at liberty *to dispose of it in any way* since it is not his to dispose of.

J.H.T. has that kind and courteous manner of expressing himself that particularly fits him for this rather difficult task. I have no knowledge where our friend J.H.T. is at the present moment, but am looking for his return from Paris.

Thine very sincerely,
Edward Newman.

To George Stacey Gibson.
Saffron Walden.

P.S. I believe the amount of subscriptions promised is 819£ but an exact list (amounts and names) is kept at No. 9 Devonshire Street and I have requested my son to show it to everyone whom he knows, if desiring to see it; please call and inspect it when convenient.

Consequent upon appointment of the Trustees, Newman prepared the following letter and leaflet, which gave a list of sums already subscribed, for distribution to those people who he thought would like to contribute:—

7, York Grove, Peckham.
London S.E.
My dear Sir,

It is my painful task to state that now, towards the close of a life devoted to the science of Natural History, more particularly the Ornithology and Entomology of the British Islands, my valued friend, Henry Doubleday, of Epping, has fallen into pecuniary difficulties.

As a matter of duty he gives up everything to his creditors, but when their claims have been satisfied he will be left entirely without income and has no prospect of profitable employment.

Under these circumstances a few of his friends propose to raise two distinct funds:

The *1st*, for purchasing, in the names of the Trustees* such portions of his Natural History collections and books as he may elect to retain, under his own control and management, for reference and study.

The *2nd*, as an annual subscription, to be paid to him quarterly, and sufficient for his maintenance in the simple manner in which he has hitherto been living:

In furtherance of these objects the undermentioned gentlemen have consented to receive subscriptions:

J. W. Dunning Esq., 24 Old Buildings, Lincoln's Inn, W.C.

H. T. Stainton Esq., Mountsfield, Lewisham, S.E.

Samuel Stevens Esq., 28 King Street, Covent Garden, W.C.

And I have pleasure in acknowledging with gratitude the following contributions already spontaneously offered.

I am, dear Sir,

Faithfully yours,

Edward Newman

* Trustees in whose names the Collections will be purchased:
  James Hack Tuke, The Bank, Hitchin.
  George Stacey Gibson, The Bank, Saffron Walden.
  Joseph Gurney Barclay, 54 Lombard Street, London.

The following sums have already been offered.

	Donation £. s. d.	*Annual Subscription* £. s. d.
Backhouse, Edward G.	25.—.—.	5.—.—.
Barclay, J. Gurney	100.—.—.	
Barclay, H. F.	5.—.—.	
Beck, Mrs.	2.—.—.	
Beck, Ernest Esq.	5.—.—.	
Bowman, Miss	10.—.—.	
Buxton, Lady and friend	140.—.—.	
Buxton, Mrs.	25.—.—.	
Doubleday, W. & H.	40.—.—.	
Dunning, J. W. Esq.	25.—.—.	10.—.—.
Gibson, Mrs.	50.—.—.	

Gibson, George Stacey	50.—.—.		
Godlee, Rickman Esq.	2.—.—.		
Hanson, Samuel Esq.		20.—.—.	
Hewitson, W. C. Esq.	25.—.—.	10.—.—.	
Head, Albert H. Esq.	3. 3.—.		
Harrison, Smith Esq.	21.—.—.		
Hurnard, James Esq.	20.—.—.	10.—.—.	
Lister, Arthur Esq.	21.—.—.		
Newman, Edward			
Pease, Joseph Esq.	50.—.—.		
Pease, J. W. Esq. M.P.	50.—.—.		
Sharples, Joseph Esq.	10.—.—.		
Smith, Richard Esq.	50.—.—.		
Stainton, H. T. Esq.	100.—.—.		50.—.—.
Stevens, Samuel Esq.			5.—.—.
Tindall, W. H. Esq.	5.—.—.		
Tuke, James Hack Esq.			

The appointed Trustees were successful in buying the collections of insects and some books either at the auction held on 23rd August 1871, at the Cock Hotel at Epping, which was directly opposite Doubleday's house, or more likely, privately. It appears that it was mainly his collection of English and foreign birds, consisting of 173 lots,[192] which was disposed of by the auctioneer, Mr. George Hine, although shells and fossils were included.

Doubleday had been home for several months when the sale took place, and it must have been a sad day indeed for him to witness the disposal of his collection, but he was doubtless heartened by the knowledge that most of his birds went into the homes of friends. As a matter of interest the names of the chief buyers were:—

Ashmead, F. Bond, William Borrer, F.L.S. of Cowfold, Horsham, Sussex; David Christy; J. H. Gurney (Jnr.), F.Z.S. etc. of Keswick Hall, Norwich; J. E. Harting, F.L.S., F.Z.S. of the Linnean Society, Burlington House, W.; Arthur Lister, J.P. of Sycamore House, Leytonstone (most of Lister's specimens are now in the Essex Field Club Museums); A. H. Smee (these specimens were also subsequently acquired by the Essex Field Club Museums), and Septimus Warner of Hoddesdon, Hertfordshire.

And so Doubleday was once more settled in his old home at Epping, the few months in the Retreat having proved extremely beneficial to him, although he was by no means restored physically: he suffered grievously from rheumatism when in the Retreat and after his return, but mentally he was much more able to deal with his problems, and he was ever anxious to express his gratitude for the release from the dire spectre of poverty.

HIS LAST ILLNESS AND TRIBUTES TO HIS LIFE AND WORK

He died on 29th June 1875 at his home, after an illness which his friends hoped was only a more than usually severe attack. Newman, who himself died just 12 months later, wrote to a friend on the day after Doubleday's death:

'Our poor friend Doubleday is dead. He died yesterday morning at 7 o'clock and without much suffering; for the last few days there had been no prospect of his recovery. With him has died a larger amount of natural history knowledge than has ever been possessed by any one of our countrymen. What a pity that it should be lost for ever. He was so reluctant to write that I believe he has left no documents behind him that will bear any evidence of the amount of his knowledge.'

Newman's great sense of loss was shared by many of his fellow naturalists and friends, and tributes to his work and life were paid by numerous people and scientific journals. Stainton, with whom Doubleday had so often met in friendly argument, spoke appreciatively of his entomological labours, particularly of his great service in correcting the nomenclature of British Lepidoptera; this was at the meeting of the Entomological Society of London, in July 1875, when the death of Doubleday, who was an Original Member, was announced by the President, Sir Sidney Smith Saunders.[193] The South London Entomological Society, which added his name to the list of Patrons in 1872, passed a unanimous resolution expressing deep regret at his death; and a copy of this Minute, which read as follows, was forwarded to Newman: 'This meeting desires to record the deep regret felt by the members present at the death of the late Mr. Henry Doubleday, whose services to Entomology have been of immense value for many years past, and whose invariable kindness has endeared him to all who have known him.'

Newman's note on the death of Doubleday in the *Entomologist* contained, as might be expected, much praise, even describing him as without exception the first Entomologist this country has produced. An extravagant claim for his friend, perhaps, but nevertheless true in the respect that he was undoubtedly the first in Britain to use such great powers of observation in the life histories of insects although he left much purely scientific examination to others.

Newman, in this notice of August 1875, also mentioned that Doubleday's house and outbuildings, furniture and books were all sold. It will be recalled that his collections of lepidoptera were placed in the hands of Trustees some years earlier, and Newman reported that no decision had been made for their disposal; although various propositions were made, the Trustees, however, did not agree with them.

The funeral was, like his life, simple and strictly after the manner of Friends: impressive in its simplicity, in a time when outward shows of sympathy were commonly considered essential; no black hat-bands were worn, no pall used, although the plain oak coffin carried by six bearers, bore a wreath.[194] A numerous gathering of friends, mainly scientific persons from various parts of England followed the cortège the short distance from his house to the Friends' Burial Ground at the rear of the little Meeting House, only a few hundred yards away.[195] At the brief service Bevan Braithwaite, a Quaker solicitor, ministered, and among the names of others present occur those of Miller Christy, Winslow, Pearson, Tweed, Sweet and Metcalf.

The plain headstone mellowing with age, marking his last resting place, can be seen in the small secluded, grass-covered burial ground at Epping, among those of several others of his family. The inscription reads very simply:—

Henry Doubleday
died
29th of 6th Month
1875
Aged 66 Years.

ON HAVING HIS LIKENESS TAKEN

What did Doubleday look like? Well, we have one or two photographs, which he was persuaded to have taken at the request of friends, from one of which an oil painting was made which passed some months after his death to the Bethnal Green Museum, with his insect collections. This portrait was transferred, with the collections, in due course to South Kensington, as will be mentioned later, and was almost certainly painted from the photograph taken about 1857 which was published in the *Entomologist* obituary notice in 1877. The previously unpublished one which is reproduced facing page one, was probably taken in April 1863, and referred to by Doubleday in a letter to Stainton dated October 23rd of that year, in which he thanked Stainton for sending him a portrait of the entomologist Zeller:—

'Last Spring in consequence of a letter which I received from Paris I went to Maull and Polyblank's[196] but I was very unwell at the time—they took a portrait and printed a few off and I sent one to Paris and gave one or two more away—but the operator wished me call again—I had a long chat with him about Photography and when he found I knew something about it he was very communicative and said he should like to try his hand again when the light was better—

About the middle of August I went to London with Miss Dix who had been staying several weeks with us and was going home on that day—we went to Maull and Polyblanks but they happened to be very busy—they however took a portrait of Maria and would have taken another of me but they detained us so long before they began that there was not time—as there was only about an hour before the Ipswich train started—I was sorry it happened so as I am not often in London and the light was good as you will see by one of Miss Dix which I will enclose—of course *it* possesses no interest to you except as a pretty good specimen of Photography. As it is very uncertain about my being in London I will get Maull and Polyblank's to print a few more of mine and send you one as soon as I get them . . .'

The following month Doubleday was able to send the photograph to Stainton, and in the meantime Stainton had sent his own portrait to Doubleday, who praised it enthusiastically. The slow journey to London and the long sitting necessary for the likeness to be taken must have been quite an irksome experience, although one full of interest for Doubleday who himself was an early experimenter. It is said that he attempted photography of insects, although no record exists of their use by him in correspondence for identification purposes.

Neither of the two photographs reflects his kindly and generous disposition, but perhaps the photographs themselves may be inadequate; for one, published with the *Entomologist* obituary notice, the editor, John Carrington, was obliged to insert a notice in the February issue advising that the biographical notice of Henry Doubleday with a *Photographic Portrait* would appear in the March issue, although it was intended for February 'but the weather has proved unsuitable for Photography'. The one reproduced facing page one was taken when he was unwell, as he mentioned in his letter to Stainton.

Very frequently portraits of Friends who achieve distinction either within the Society or outside were hung in the London Friends' Institute, but in Henry's case no portrait appears to have been available,[197] although a brief account of his life was printed in the publication by a Committee of the Friends' Institute of 13 Bishops-gate Street Without, dated 1888, entitled *Biographical Catalogue, being an account of the Lives of Friends and others whose Portraits are in the London Friends' Institute*. Another Quaker publication however, in a Supplement dated 1893, mentioned that Henry's portrait, in oils, was in the Bethnal Green Museum, together with his collections and undoubtedly it was the one which was deposited in due course at South Kensington. The publication referred to was in two volumes, by Joseph Smith,[198] dated 1867, entitled *A descriptive Catalogue of Friends Books or Books written by Members of the Society of Friends, commonly called Quakers, from their first rise to the present time, interspersed with critical remarks, and Occasional Biographical Notices, and including all writings by authors before joining, and by those after having left the Society, whether adverse or not, as far as is known*. This book followed on that of John Whiting, published in 1708, which was long out of print.

THE DOUBLEDAY COLLECTIONS

The splendid collections of insects were deposited on loan with the Bethnal Green Museum[199] by the '1871' Trustees (Tuke, Gibson and Barclay) early in 1876, who doubtless took into consideration Doubleday's own request, and listened to the views of other ento-mologists and societies.[200]

The period of the original loan was five years, and in 1881 this was extended for a further period of five years. The exact terms of the Trust upon which the collection was received in 1876 were apparently not defined, or at any rate when enquiries were made some years later the British Museum authorities were not aware of them, and in 1915, when it was felt appropriate that these collections should be housed at South Kensington,[201] the authorities did not feel they had any obligation to enquire further into the nature of the Trust, which did not appear to have renewed the loan after 1886. We may therefore be content that they have found a rightful home in the British Museum (Natural History), where they may be inspected by anyone interested who enquires after the 'Doubleday Collection'. By 1915 the last survivor of the Trustees, Barclay, had died and consequently there was no alternative but to place the collections on 'permanent loan' where they may be easily consulted and are carefully looked after; and this would doubtless have been his own wish.

Of the specimens themselves it may be briefly mentioned that they are contained in four cabinets, two forming the British Collection and two the European. The two former cabinets consist of forty drawers and sixty drawers, and the foreign insects in cabinets of twenty-four drawers and seven drawers. Shortly after receiving the collections (February 1876) catalogues were published,[202] prefaced by the following note:—

'The well-known Collections of Lepidoptera left by the late Mr. Henry Doubleday, of Epping, have, in accordance with his wish, been deposited on loan in the Bethnal Green branch of the South Kensington Museum by his Executors, Messrs. J. H. Tuke, G. S. Gibson and J. G. Barclay, and with the view of adding to the usefulness of the loan, the Lords of the Committee of Council on Education have directed catalogues of their contents to be published.

They have been prepared by Mr. Andrew Murray, F.L.S. and collated with the Collections by Mr. A. B. Farn.'

Further general information referring to the British specimens was given in the catalogue as follows:—

'This catalogue is a mere record of the contents of each drawer of Mr. Doubleday's Collection, in the exact order in which he left them. It will be found that the order in which the species succeed each other is not always the same as that in his published *Systematic List*. This generally arises from the difference in the numbers of individuals shown of each species, which required a little management to make them suit the drawers without leaving blanks and breaking up the genus into more drawers than is absolutely necessary; but there are also differences of arrangement which seem to indicate an alteration or modification of his views on certain points.'

Advice regarding the European insects, in a separate catalogue, reads as follows:—

'This collection was left by Mr. Doubleday in separate boxes, in which it was not arranged either according to his own system, or apparently on any determined general system. In transferring it to cabinets for better preservation, it has been thought best to arrange it in the order which is now most generally adopted by European Lepidopterists—*viz*: that followed by Staudinger in his *List*. With a few exceptions, which are noted as they occur, this has been done with the genera and families and in the generic determination of species, but in other respects the species stand in the order in which Doubleday left them.

The Collection is in fine condition, but, as in all large collections, there are occasional damaged specimens. These have been noted where the damage is important, but minor flaws, such as the absence of a leg or single antenna, have not been specified.'

In the notice in the *Dictionary of National Biography*, Miller Christy said that these collections had probably never been excelled in richness or in variety.[203] Certainly no-one could have bestowed greater care than Doubleday in the setting of the specimens, and the standard he achieved is all the more remarkable considering the illness which affected his hand over a long period of his life.

EPILOGUE

And so this modest man, who wished for nothing but a quiet country life where he could study the rich wild life with which he was surrounded in Epping, achieved perhaps more than he knew, leaving his mark for ever in the annals of the natural history of this country. The memorial card which Newman distributed in remembrance of his great friend bore the following verse:

'Non Sanguine et Genere insignis,
Sed quod majus
Propria Virtute Illustris.
De Opibus Titulisque obtinendis

Parum sollicitus,
Haec potius mereri voluit quam adipisci:
Dum sub Privato Lare, suâ Sorte contentus
(Fortunâ lautiori dignus) consenuit.
In Rebus aliis sibi modum facilè imposuit,
In Studiis nullum.'

'Not outstanding for birth or lineage, but what is more, remarkable
for his private character. He cared little for gaining wealth or title;
he preferred to deserve them rather than to acquire them. Worthy
of a more distinguished fate, he grew old beneath his own roof,
contented with his lot. Whilst in other matters he easily set limits
upon himself, he set none in the pursuit of his studies.'[204]

BIBLIOGRAPHY AND NOTES

Abbreviations which have been used include the following:—

Annals and Magazine of Natural History—Ann. Mag. nat. Hist.

Entomologist—Ent.

Entomologist's Monthly Magazine—Ent. mon. Mag.

Essex Record Office—E.R.O.

Essex Naturalist—Essex Nat.

Essex Review—Essex Rev.

London Naturalist—Lond. Nat.

Magazine of Natural History—Mag. nat. Hist.

Natural History Magazine—Nat. Hist. Mag.

Phytologist—Phyt.

Victoria County History—V.C.H.

Zoologist—Zool.

1. Ward, Bernard T., 1956 *Essex Nat.* 29 pt 5.

2. Mays, R. H., 1961 *Essex Nat.* 30 pt 5.

3. The name is widespread but, I am informed, met with particularly in Northumberland and Leicestershire, in the Belvoir area of which the Doubledays were principally country builders, so Mr. Ernest Doubleday, O.B.E., who was the County Planning Officer for Hertfordshire advises me. The name can be traced there for over 400 years. As was usual in earlier times, the surname was spelled in a variety of ways, the clerk writing it down as he heard it pronounced; for example in the Westminster Calendar of Wills 1504–1858, in 1620 the name of E. Dowbleday occurs, as well as the more usual spelling in 1642 and 1663. Similarly the will of Joan Dubleday, St. Martins, Ludgate, was proved in the Court of the Archdeaconry of London on 12th Sept. 1564, and in Somerset House is the will of 'Elizabeth Doubleday, otherwise Doubledee, formerly Ellis, of Middlesex', proved in November 1774. (F.392).

4. C. W. Bardsley, 1901 *A Dictionary of English and Welsh Surnames*, Henry Frowde, London.

5. This house was quite a large property, the land being of the Manor of Epping Bury, and we know from old records that in 1831 the house was valued for rating at £26 per annum, Benjamin paying £2.12.0d, i.e. a rate of two shillings.
   Following Henry Doubleday's death in 1875, the grocery business was taken over by Joseph Hills, who ran it for many years. These fine premises were used continuously as a grocer's shop until the building was demolished in 1966, when the International Stores erected a modern self-service shop on the site. In the wall of the new store, facing Buttercross Lane, Epping Urban District Council have fixed a plaque, reminding passers by that one of Epping's most distinguished inhabitants spent his life in a house on that site.

6. Durrant's *Handbook for Essex*, 1887, incorrectly gives 1807, as do many reference books. Relatives of the Epping Doubledays were engaged in similar business elsewhere in Essex, that in Coggeshall being carried on until the

late 1950's, albeit on a rather restricted scale, by Thomas and his sister Edith Doubleday, who were the last of the family with close relationship to Henry with whom we are particularly concerned. In later years at Coggeshall only drapery was sold, but the extensive premises in the centre of the town showed the importance and extent of the business in years gone by. The ancient building which they occupied has now, alas, been demolished, following its sale consequent upon Thomas Doubleday's death at an advanced age in January 1961; he survived his sister, who was a few years his senior, by a year or so; neither married.

7. Raistrick, A., 1950. *Quakers in Science and Industry, being an Account of the Quaker Contributions to Science and Industry during the 17th and 18th Centuries.* (Bannisdale Press, London).

8. It is interesting to note that about the time when Benjamin's parents set up business in Epping, there was, in 1741, a Thomas Doubleday, described as a grocer, trading in Bishopsgate Street, London (*The Universal Pocket Companion*), and Ralph Doubleday, an indico (sic) merchant, was in business in the 1750's and 1760's in Fish Street Hill, London. (*Mortimer's Universal Director*).

9. *Essex Nat.* 1920 (XXII).

10. Percy Thompson F.L.S. was the author of an article in *Essex Nat.* 1925 (XXI) entitled '*The Willingales of Loughton*', which was reprinted as a pamphlet by the Essex Field Club. One of the Club's keenest supporters, he was, during his 47 years membership, Secretary for over 30, for many years Curator of its Museum, and Editor of the Club's publication, the *Essex Nat.* He died aged 86 in 1953.

Edward North Buxton's book '*Epping Forest*' (1884, Edw. Stanford, London) contains a good account of the prolonged legal battle; his own efforts and generosity resulted in the preservation of the nearby forests of Hainault and Hatfield (also known as Takeley Forest) as open spaces for all time. Buxton, who died in 1924 was a Verderer of Epping Forest.

The Corporation of London, which understandably was immensely popular following the legal decision, had the support of a number of local societies, particularly the Haggerston Entomological Society (the forerunner of the London Natural History Society) and the East London Entomological and Botanical Society (later known as the Eastern Entomological Society). The Corporation members, on 28th November 1874 triumphantly toured the Forest, finishing up with a dinner at the Castle Hotel, Woodford.

Punch, in a more serious mood, published the following poem in 1928, recalling this epic struggle for common rights:—

Epping Forest

One Willingale of Loughton—blesséd be his name!—
Stood beside a hornbeam, lopping of the same;
The lord of Loughton Manor bidding him begone,
Willingale said several things and Willingale went on,
And when I stand by Loughton Camp and look on Debden Slade
I think upon one Willingale and how his billhook played;
For Willingale, a labourer, by lopping of a tree
Kept houses off the Forest for men like you and me.

A man who lived by Woodford, he found upon a day
A fence up in Lord's Bushes across the bridle-way;
He went to no solicitor nor Counsel of the Crown,
But, being of the Manor, he pulled the fencing down;

93

And out beside Fox Burrows, breathing of the spring,
I will still remember the man who did this thing:
For Great Monk Wood and Little and Copley Plain were trim
And narrow streets like Walthamstow except for men like him.

Before you climb Woodredden Hill to reach the Verderer's Ride
I bid you mark how London would not be denied,
But, holding Wanstead graveyard, claimed common for a cow,
And, champion of all common rights, thrust into the row;
How, like a noble city, for three long years she fought,
Till Jessel, Master of the Rolls, gave judgment as he ought
And nine miles out from Aldgate Pump she kept the Forest free,
Untouched, untamed, a pleasant place for men like you and me.

11. Isaac Payne's school apparently enjoyed a wide reputation for providing a sound and liberal education: not only members of the Society of Friends who naturally preferred to send their sons there, as Isaac was a member of the Society, but also many local and London business men. They spoke highly of their old tutor, Isaac Payne, who was, it is said, held in vast respect by them all. Dr. Benjamin Winstone (1819–1907), who is mentioned elsewhere as the author of the book on the *Epping and Ongar Highway Trust*, was educated there, and was almost the last survivor of his pupils: a versatile man, Winstone practised as a surgeon and headed a company which manufactured the special ink used by the Bank of England for their notes—a firm which is still in existence: he was also the local historian of his home town, Epping, an archaeologist, and author of several books (*Essex Rev.*1907 (XVI)). The last of Payne's pupils, however, was another Quaker (Winstone was of Quaker origin both on his mother's and his father's side), Septimus Warner of Hoddesdon in Hertfordshire, a contemporary schoolfellow of almost the same age. Many of the Warner family received their early education at Isaac Payne's, Septimus' four elder brothers all attending the school together: one brother, Robert achieved distinction as a botanist and engineer, but is best known for founding, in 1840, the United Kingdom Provident Institution, of which he was Chairman for no less than 50 years. He died on 17th December 1896, aged 81 (*Essex Rev.* 1897 VI). Names of other scholars included T. Mashitor, W. Barnard of Sawbridgeworth, Dr. Brickwell, Masterman and Harrip (*Essex Rev.* 1905 XIV). The successor to Isaac Payne at the school was Dr. Usmar. Septimus Warner, who was the seventh son of John Warner, also of Hoddesdon, attended not only Isaac Payne's school but was accepted as a pupil of the Doubledays' relative, Henry Smith, who farmed successfully at Great Bardfield Hall in Essex. In 1847 Henry Smith married John Warner's elder daughter, and died in 1864, leaving a large family of eleven children. Another of Doubleday's Quaker relatives was Joseph Smith, also a Payne pupil, who farmed at Pattiswick Hall in Essex from 1836 to 1865, when he married and moved to Great Saling in the same county, where he died in 1904. (*Essex Rev.* 1905 XIV).

12. Deane, who in later years was in business as a chemist and druggist at Clapham Common, was born at Stratford, London, on 11th August 1807, and died on 4th April 1874, a year before Doubleday. Upon his marriage in 1843 he left the Society of Friends (Quakers), possibly because of the then strict Quaker rule of 'disowning' upon 'marrying out'. Edward Newman, who composed Deane's obituary notice in the *Entomologist*, gathered his facts from Deane's autobiography, which he said he had before him. (*Ent.* 1874, VII).

94

13. *Essex Weekly News.* December 1894. According to the late C. B. Sworder, a member of an old-established Epping family, who collected items of local interest, the Doubleday boys, after mentioning the year (1819) being the 59th of the reign of George III, gave the following list of principal residents:—'W. Cumming, H. Partridge, C. Healey, J. Payne, D. R. McNab, Thos. Squire, J. Kankin, Jo. Wolton, B. Doubleday, Thos. Coell, I. Lepine, R. B. Hayward, E. Griffin, R. Stokes, H. Binikis'—adding—'Silver coin in circulation—Crowns, half-crowns, shillings and sixpences. Copper do: Two-penny pieces, Penny pieces, half-pence, and farthings. The Gold coins are guineas 21/-, half-guineas 10/6, 1/3 of a guinea 7/-, Sovereigns 20/-, half do: 10/-.' (Sworder MSS, *E.R.O.*).

14. *Essex Rev.* 1928 Vol. 37.

15. Edward Doubleday, who lived in Harrington Square, Westminster, died on 14th Nov, 1849 aged 38. Mary Doubleday, his mother, died on June 28th 1846 aged 67, and his father Benjamin died on Dec. 24th 1847, aged 76. (*Friends' Annual Monitor* 1846, 1847, 1849).

16. Information taken from '*Minutes of Epping & Ongar Highway Trust*' by Benjamin Winstone, 1891. These minutes were extracted from the Minute Books kept at the offices of Windus & Trotter, at Epping. John Windus was Clerk to the Trustees when the Trust terminated in 1870. Included in the book, which was published for private circulation, was a full copy of the Act. Benjamin Doubleday, upon his appointment of Treasurer, was required to give a bond for £1,000 and to find two sureties for £500 each.
   The inaugural meeting of the Trust was on the first Tuesday in May 1769 at Epping Place, which was an inn, the house of Grace Stokes, the Act providing for further meetings at any house upon the highway, at most convenient dates. The first meeting drew a large attendance, and although later meetings were not so well attended, the Trustees appeared to be progressive and generally speaking they carried out their duties efficiently and energetically. The tolls were vested in the Trustees by virtue of the Act, and to give some idea of the amount collected by the Trust, it is interesting to note that in 1793 the tolls were leased to Mr. Joseph Usherwood for a period of three years for £1,140 per annum, payable in quarterly instalments. Mr. Usherwood, however, made a very bad bargain, and at the end of only one year, from Michaelmas to Midsummer, the Epping Turnpike had produced but £579.7.0d and the Ongar Turnpike only £94.10.9d. As a result the Trustees with characteristic generosity passed a Minute, 'It appearing to the Trustees to be improper for a publick trust to profit by the ruin of an individual, it was resolved that the benefit of the Clause in the Act 9th: George III, which gives the Trustees a power of revoking former contracts, be taken'.
   During the life of the Trust, a number of Acts of Parliament were passed affecting its organisation and function: particularly the Act of 1811 which renewed the Turnpike Acts for a further 21 years, and made provision for amendments to the toll charges and prevention of certain nuisances. Eleven years later the General Highway Act was passed, more particularly entitled '*An Act to amend the general laws now in being for regulating Turnpike Roads in that part of Great Britain called England*', and arising out of this, a local Act was passed in the same year, 1822, to be effective for 21 years, for more effectually repairing the roads between Harlow, Woodford, Epping and Writtle. It was in connection with this Act that the Trust were liable for certain bills, one being for 12 guineas to cover expenses incurred by 'Mr. Jessop, Mr. Smith and Mr. Doubleday and coach hire, as witnesses attending in the House of Lords, and Commons, and at the Chelmsford Sessions.'

17. The Trust's Turnpike passes took the form of discs about an inch in diameter and a quarter of an inch thick: made of burnt clay, they were stamped with various letters for identification. (*Essex Rev.* 1923, XXXII).

18. *Essex Rev.* 1928 XXXVII contained a photograph of this forgery. Almost every town of any size had its own private bank in the 19th Century, many of which issued their own paper currency, and it was inevitable that numerous forged notes should find their way into circulation: this occurred despite the severe penalties for forgery—in fact between 1700 and 1818 it is recorded that 140 executions for this crime took place (*Book of Dates*, 1862. Griffin Bohn).

19. So far as the Coggeshall branch is concerned no Doubleday appears in the 1577 or 1652 lists of persons engaged in Coggeshall's staple business, cloth-making, nor in the lists of clothier's or other trader's tokens which were issued in the second half of the 17th Century in Coggeshall (Beaumont, 1890, *History of Coggeshall*), although in the Parish Register at Coggeshall, the Notice of Marriage of William Doubledue to Elizabeth Hills in 1645 is entered.

20. In view of the title 'Mr.', not normally used by Quakers, could this member of the family have not belonged to the Society?

21. These seven inns were at Chelmsford, Wrabness, Bocking, Weeley, Wivenhoe, Great Bromley and Coggeshall. Danbury also boasted a beer-house of that name. The Demi-Moor, whose supporters were 'two young Moors proper, wreathed about the loins with tobacco leaves vert', which formed the Black Boy inn sign, was taken from the arms of the Tobacco-pipe Makers' Company, incorporated in 1663. The Chelmsford inn probably gave its name to others in the county, for this impressive building was of considerable importance: it was formerly owned by the powerful and wealthy de Vere family, the Earls of Oxford, who built the Castle at Hedingham in 1130 and occupied it for nearly 600 years, until 1703: they naturally stayed at the Black Boy when passing through Chelmsford on their journeys to London, but in earlier times it was known as the Crown. After standing for five centuries the Black Boy was demolished in 1857 (*Essex Rev.* 1897 VI). J. Ryland made his well-known engraving of this inn in 1762, from David Ogborne's view, which showed a Judge's Procession passing under the great beam which projected 33 feet to a post set up in the middle of the street for its support, and from which the Black Boy sign was swinging. (*Essex Rev.* 1900 IX, *Essex Rev.* 1895 IV, *Gentleman's Magazine* 1845, 2nd Ser. Vol. 24, *Essex Rev.* 1916 XXV, Miller Christy 1887, *Trade Signs of Essex.* Mention of the inn is in the immortal *Pickwick Papers*). The destruction of this inn must have been regretted by many people, for it would appear to have been quite progressive, providing baths in addition to those available elsewhere in the High Street and carrying on its business as a coaching inn up to the time of its demolition. The sign of the Black Boy was doubtless a familiar one in many cities and towns throughout the country and probably most of all in London. John Ray, writing to Sloane in the 17th Century addressed his letters 'For Dr. Hans Sloane, to be left at Mr. Wilkinson's, a bookseller, at the Black Boy, over against St. Dunstan's Church, in Fleet Street,' and again writing from Black Notley in Essex, to Edward Lluyd 'at Mr. Haughton's at the Black Boy in Chancery Lane'. This letter to Lluyd is dated 1689 and may be found in the Bodleian Library (G. S. Boulger *Unpublished material relating to John Ray*).
At Coggeshall, where the Doubledays were well established, the Black Boy inn was situated near Market Hill and was known in 1708 as the Corner House, but by 1803, if not earlier, it became the Black Boy.

The 'Quaker Town' of Saffron Walden (so named because of the number of people belonging to that religious Society who resided there and who during the 19th Century took a prominent part in the affairs of the town) was also not without its cheerful sign of the Black Boy: from time to time inns were converted into private houses and vice versa, an example being a dwelling house which became the Black Boy in the reign of Queen Elizabeth. (C. B. Rowntree, 1951, *Saffron Walden—Then and Now*). It was presumably this same inn which became the favourite resort of the Saffron Walden townspeople in later years: included in the accounts of a local tradesman, preserved in Saffron Walden Museum, is an interesting one dated 1650, reading as follows:—'Mr. John Turner, for the Penthouses about the Black Boy, VIII s'. 'Penthouses' were described as 'sheds hanging out aslope from the main walls'. Another reference to the same inn occurs in the Corporation records, dated March 27th 1682 'Spent at the Black Boy 12 pence', and a little later we read the sum of 4 shillings and 6 pence was 'spent at the Black Boy with the Chamberlains when we assessed the fines on the Quakers' (*Essex Rev.* 1917 XXVI). Quakers figured prominently, of course, in early Saffron Walden records, and many instances may be quoted in which they were prosecuted for holding their illegal Meetings: George Whitehead (1636–1723) for example served several imprisonments for his beliefs, and was placed in the stocks at Saffron Walden and whipped, and in 1664 '3 shillings was paid at the Bell when Quakers were committed'. The Bell was converted into a private house by William Impey in 1818 and is now the site of Saffron Walden cattle market.

Inns were primarily for the use of travellers but in those days they were important meeting places. Essex roads were undoubtedly at their best and busiest in the two decades after 1820, but in many places the disuse of coaching meant they were far less used and this in consequence meant that the status of inns had considerably deteriorated by the end of the 19th Century. So far as the roads in the vicinity of Epping were concerned, although Sir James McAdam, who was appointed Surveyor to the Epping and Ongar Highway Trust in 1830, was responsible for great improvements to them, the coming of the railway age ensured a great decline in both goods and passenger traffic after 1840. Epping inns at the end of the 19th Century had even earned the reputation of being 'little more than tippling-houses, or drinking places for the poorer classes' for which 'the upper stratum has but little connection with them, beyond receiving their rents', as one author wrote.

22. The other Epping inns in 1789 were the White Lion, Bell, Cock (John and Mary Archer kept this in 1636), Swan, Black Lion, Cock & Magpie, Green Man, Globe, George, Rose & Crown, Thatched House, White Hart, Harp, Sun, Chequers and Epping Place. (*Essex Rev.* 1902 XI) It was in 1551 that alehouses were first licensed, twenty-four flourishing in Epping by 1681, although no record appears to exist showing the date of the first alehouse there; however, in 1631 there were five 'inn-holders' and ten 'victulars' in Epping. No less than forty-four alehouses and inns existed within the parish boundary in 1681, the increase from 1631 being attributed to a large extent by the employment of labourers on the new road which was constructed between Thornwood Common and London, through Epping (*Essex Rev.* 1923 XXXII). The landlords chose colourful names for Epping inns, among the most picturesque being Peacock Pye, Cucking Stool, Leather Bottle and Salt Box: the name of the inn at which Samuel Pepys spent a night in 1660, which he mentions in his Diary, is unfortunately not known, but it could not have been the best-known of all Epping inns, Epping Place, for it was said to be first leased as an inn in 1758; this was the inn which was the first

meeting place of the Epping and Ongar Highway Trust, in 1769, then described as the 'house of Grace Stokes'. Forty-seven years later, in 1816, it was owned by Richard Stokes—apparently a most successful landlord, for he was also inn-keeper of the White Hart at Woodford, and had another inn on the Newmarket to London road, probably at Harlow. His stables at the White Hart held twenty post-horses, looked after by his horsekeeper, James Francis; later on he moved to Epping Place, where he had a similar number to look after (*Highways and Byways of Essex*, 1955, E.R.O.). Although first becoming an inn in 1758, the house was built so it is recorded, by Sir Moyle Finch in 1557 as a private residence and was known as Winchelsea House. Cary, in his '*Itinerary*' said, in 1821, that it was the only house in Epping to provide horses and carriages; some ten coaches arrived daily from London and about the same number travelling in the opposite direction, and in addition several others, all four-in-hand, passed daily through to other destinations, for it was a most convenient stopping place for breakfast for the London to Cambridge coaches. The names of the main coaches halting at Epping Place were The Fakenham, Norwich, Cambridge 'Times', Cambridge Coach, Bury Coach, Swaffham Coach, Magnet, Walden Coach, Thetford Coach and the Harlow Coach. In 1844 it ceased as a Coaching Station when the last licensee, Mrs. Caroline Stokes, gave up the licence; its forty-two horses were sold together with harness and coaches, and among the contents of the inn which were disposed of were some 231 dozen of port, 5 dozen of sherry and 2 dozen of champagne. The Centenary volume of the *Trans. of the Essex Archaeological Society* (1960) contains a fascinating account of the changes seen by this outstanding Epping house and of its various owners and tenants. (It was kept by a member of the Stokes family throughout its life as an inn). (J. H. Holmes, vol. XXV, Pt. III, New Series).

23. Thomas Story was a frequent visitor to Ury with its 2,000 acre estate, for he was a friend of Mrs. Barclay and later with her son, Robert. It is rather confusing that the same Christian names were carried down over the generations, but it appears that it was Christian, (another daughter of Robert Barclay senr., apparently sister to John Doubleday's wife) who married Alexander Jeffery, whose son was named Thomas after Thomas Story (Emily E. Moore, 1947, *Travelling with Thomas Story*, Letchworth Printers).
The 'famous and honourable' Robert Barclay (1648–90) was of course 'The Apologist', who was the 2nd Laird of Urie; The wife of John Doubleday with whom Story stayed, was named Mollison Barclay, the sister of another Robert Barclay (1699–1760), the 4th Laird. After the death of John Doubleday it is recorded that Mollison married a man named Strettel. Capt. Robert Barclay-Allardice, who died in 1854 was the last Laird of Urie.

24. Charles Wright, 1896, *Nonconformity in Epping* writes 'A Friends Meeting House was built in Epping about the middle of last century. It was an unusually picturesque building without, but of the usual type of neatness within. It had a rustic portico or verandah all round it, and was covered by a thatched roof extending beyond its walls down to the pillars which also supported it. It stood on the site of the present stables at Theydon Grove, when an open common with a pond (called Butler's Weir) and some cottages, reached up to the site of the present mansion. About 1845, the time of the enclosure, through the instrumentality of Benjamin Doubleday then about 60 years of age, these old cottages were pulled down, and the old meeting also, the present building being included in the enclosed portion now forming the Grove grounds . . . '
Wright also refers to Benjamin Doubleday's shop as a 'curious emporium'.

25. Friends House Library, Minutes 1830–1845.
26. This William Doubleday was probably the one mentioned in a Deed of 1851 in connection with the Charity known as Thomas Paycocke's. Paycocke, who was a wealthy Coggeshall clothier, in his will dated 20th December 1580, left, among other things, £200 to be spent on 'the purchase of free lands and tenements' and the profits to be distributed among the poor people of Coggeshall. The Executors of the will, which included one R. Benyon, were to convey the property so acquired to 'ten of the headboroughs of Coggeshall or more and their heirs upon the said trusts'. No Doubleday appears among the first list of headboroughs appointed following Benyon's first Conveyance of 17th March 1584, but coming to more recent times, William Doubleday's name is listed with thirteen others, in a Deed dated 26th December 1851; a further Deed of 15th June 1887 contains the name of Edward Doubleday, by which time only two of the 1851 headboroughs had survived. (Beamont 1890 *Hist. of Coggeshall*).
27. The Society of Friends having no paid Minister, appoint, for their meetings, a Clerk who may best be described as 'Leader', or Chairman—someone who is responsible for the right-ordering and well-being of the meeting.
28. *Essex Rev.* 1918 XXVII.
29. *Essex Nat.* 1894 VIII.
30. A Directory of 1838 also describes Benjamin Doubleday as a tea-dealer. The Doubledays also made tallow candles and soap on the premises, and when the house was demolished in 1966, a cauldron, probably used for this purpose, 5 feet in diameter, was found on the site.
31. The pages of the *Zoologist* in the 1850's bear ample witness to this.
32. Perhaps Dunning was reminded of the 'Man of Ross', John Kyrle (1637–1724) by the formation of the Kyrle Society, founded in his honour in 1877, two years after Doubleday's death (vide Brewer's *Dictionary of Phrase and Fable* (Cassell, n.d.)). It was in March of that year when Dunning's biographical notice in the *Entomologist* was published.
33. Thomas P. Doubleday was also a descendant of Thomas Puplett (1824–1889), an Essex Quaker, born at Layer Breton, who was a master at the Yorkshire Quaker school, Ackworth, for nearly 40 years. (1891, *Friends of a half-century* (1840–1890). Edited by Wm. Robinson. Published by Edw. Hicks (jnr.) and H. D. & R. Headley).
34. It was apparently in 1837 that the last hold-ups by highwaymen in the Epping neighbourhood occurred; on this occasion three men, one armed with a double-barrelled pistol, were unwise enough to waylay a well-known Epping solicitor, Mr. Windus, who was on his way to London one morning. His cash and watch were demanded and duly handed over. They were afterwards caught, and one man, presumably the one who was armed, was hanged (*Essex Rev.* 1923 XXXII). The Epping Forest roads, always dangerous, were particularly so in earlier times, especially, it is said, following the peace of 1698, when a large number of discharged soldiers took to marauding on the highways.
35. Henry Doubleday of Market End, Coggeshall researched into the production of Russian Comfrey (*Symphytum peregrinum*) in England with Thomas Christy (1953, L. D. Hills, *Russian Comfrey*, Faber & Faber). He is also not so well known as an inventor of a special gum for use on postage stamps, of a method of starch manufacture; and other things. It has been recorded that because of the expense he had to decline the offer of Fellowship of the Royal Society.

36. Theo. Compton, 1893: *Recollections of Tottenham Friends and the Forster family*, Edward Hicks, jnr.

37. Edward Newman recorded in *The Field* the shooting of this bird on 19th October 1858 (Vol. XII p. 357).

38. *The Spectator* of Feb. 28th 1712 and March 4th 1712 carried an advertisement stating that the seat of Sir P. Soame, Bt, at Heydon (on the borders of Essex, Hertfordshire and Cambridgeshire) was to let, 'Bustard and Pheasant abounding on it'. This is also noted in Glegg's *'Birds of Essex'* (1929). The *Victoria County History* (1903) mentions some Essex places where the birds have been seen, and usually, alas, shot, including Woodham Ferrers, West Wickham, Manningtree, Tillingham and Hatfield Broad Oak.

39. Heysham died on April 6th 1857 (*Entomologist's Weekly Intelligencer*, 1857, No. 29).

40. Robert Miller Christy, 1861–1928, eldest son of Robert Christy of Chignal St. James in Essex. Miller Christy mentioned that it was through the kindness of the Rev. H. A. Macpherson that he had the opportunity of perusing the letters. His earlier schooldays were spent at Epping, afterwards at the Quaker school of Bootham: although only a young man when Doubleday died in 1875, he had a great admiration for the Epping Quaker: other books included *Birdsnesting and Bird skinning* (1888) and *Trade Signs of Essex* (1887).

41. In a later letter to Heysham, Doubleday described an unusually light coloured Common Buzzard which a Forest keeper had shot on September 8th 1840.

42. The Pettychaps or Greater Pettychaps, a summer visitor, is now more popularly known as the Garden Warbler, and the Lesser Pettychaps as the Chiff-chaff.

43. His correspondence shows he had in no small measure the endless patience required in those days to achieve a good photograph, and was able to discuss the technical problems with professional photographers.

44. *Saffron Walden Weekly News*, January 11th, 1963.

45. *Zool.* XXII, 1864. (Letter 11.5.64).

46. Christy's *Birds of Essex*, and Buxton's *Epping Forest* also carried accounts of Doubleday's success in keeping Hawfinches.

47. Jardine's *Magazine of Zoology* 1837, I, 448.

48. Doubleday investigated the history of this bird very thoroughly—at one time it was thought to be purely migratory, but it was accepted as not being so, after he had found it all the year round at Epping. Information on the bird was, over a lengthy period, conveyed by Doubleday to various scientific journals, particularly to the *Zoologist*, as well as in private correspondence. He wrote to Heysham of its abundance in 1835 and 1836 in the Forest and of its scarcity in the following years up to 1840, because of the failure of the seed crop on the hornbeams due to cold and frosty springs: in fact in December 1837 he showed his concern at the lack of food, writing:—
'I do not know what will become of the Hawfinches this Winter as there is an entire failure of their favourite food, the seed of the hornbeam. I do not think there is a seed all through the forest and last Winter every tree was loaded. It may quite drive them away.' And so on with similar news of the Hawfinch population showing how it varied with abundance or scarcity of hornbeam seeds over the years; these birds were closely observed by both the Doubleday brothers, who were aware also of the destruction they

caused to the vegetable gardens in the district, Edward writing in 1840, 'When the young are fledged they visit the gardens near the forest in search of green peas. I have been told that last year, nearly, if not quite, thirty were killed in the garden of Colonel Conyers of Copt Hall, whose park I believe to be a favourite breeding place of this bird'. (The Conyers family formerly lived at Epping Place, converted into an inn after they left it, and referred to elsewhere as the first meeting place of the Epping and Ongar Highway Trust. They rebuilt Copt Hall in 1753). In favourable years Henry, and also his assistant James English, reported flocks of several hundred birds at a time in the Forest (*Journal of Proc. of the Essex Field Club* 1881). See also *Zool.* 1861 for Doubleday's remarks on the Hawfinch, Redshank and Lesser Tern, in '*Collected observations on the nests and eggs of British Birds*'.

49. Records were extracted as follows: 1828–1830 from the Heysham correspondence; 1831–1836, Heysham letters and *Zool.*; 1837–1838, *Zool.*; 1839–1840, Heysham letters and *Zool.*; 1841 chiefly in *Zool.*, partly Heysham letters; 1842–1843 *Zool.*; 1844 Heysham letters and *Zool.*; 1845 *Zool.*

50. More of Rev. Revett Sheppard's records may be found by consulting '*A Catalogue of the Norfolk and Suffolk birds, with remarks*', by Revett Sheppard and Wm. Whitear. *Trans. of the Linn. Soc. XV, and Ibis,* 1829, X.

51. William Doubleday King (1801–1870) was Henry's first cousin; he was a Quaker draper who lived in Sudbury, a very keen naturalist, and being a first class bird stuffer, he accumulated a large and valuable collection of British Birds. This, in due course, passed to his nephew, John Grubb of Birmingham and was preserved there in one of the rooms of the Library adjoining the Friends' Meeting House. King, connected also with the private banking firm of Alexander & Co., helped to form the Sudbury Museum, which was dispersed in 1872. T. B. Hall of Coggeshall contributed an article on this museum to the first volume of the *Zool.* in 1843. Another very keen ornithological friend of William Doubleday King was his Irish born brother-in-law, Jonathan Grubb, a Quaker corn-miller who spent his working life near Colchester, but who upon retirement spent the rest of his life at Sudbury, taking it is said, great interest in the natural history of the district.

52. These articles appeared between August 6th and Sept. 17th 1880.

53. These two Green Sandpipers were referred to by Buxton in 1884 in his *Epping Forest*. Another bird for which few Essex records existed in Doubleday's time was the Wood Sandpiper, but he was fortunate enough to have had a specimen brought to him in the following circumstances:—'On the previous Monday' he wrote to Heysham on 10th May 1840, 'a fellow celebrated for poaching brought me a Wood Sandpiper which he shot at a pond on our common. It was a female and the eggs very much enlarged. He says there were two of them, probably a pair. The one he brought in is in full summer plumage.' Yarrell mentions hearing of the occurrence from Henry Doubleday. An example of another bird of the same species, which is a rather uncommon migrant to Essex, was given by Doubleday to the Saffron Walden Museum in 1840.

54. Letter to Heysham August 24th 1832. It was in the years 1840, 1841 and 1842 that many references were made to Green Sandpipers in his correspondence.

55. When giving a list of Shetland birds, T. Edmonston in an article entitled *Fauna of Shetland* in the *Zool.*, II, 1844, gave the Common Sandpiper as a winter visitor, which was later corrected by Doubleday in the *Zool.*

101

56. Yarrell in *British Birds* 2nd Edition (1845).
57. These were shot on 4th October 1833, as mentioned in a letter to Heysham. Of this bird, which is an autumn migrant and can occasionally be seen around the coast in springtime, Miller Christy in his book commented:—'It is remarkable as the only British bird whose eggs remain undiscovered.' It was in the previous year (1832) that Doubleday noted a specimen in a collection at Colchester which had been captured on the adjacent coast, and this probably prompted his visit the following year. (1884, Buxton, *Epping Forest*).
58. *Zool.* 1851, IX.
59. They were sold for twenty-one shillings, one specimen being bought by Mr. Hope; some confusion appears to exist over the identity of this bird, as the *Victoria County History* (1903) refers to Hope's bird as a Wilson's Petrel (*Oceanites oceanicus* (*Kuhl*)), and there was nothing to prove it was the one taken in November 1840. However, Glegg in *Birds of Essex* was of the opinion that it was the same bird, and Doubleday was hardly likely to have been in error. Glegg also recorded another sea-bird, the Manx Shearwater, as having been picked up dead in an Epping garden on September 21st 1866, 'a very fat specimen', said Doubleday in the *Zool.* of that year. It was the first definite record of this bird from Essex, although Edward Doubleday reported finding a Shearwater in Epping in 1835, but he did not identify the species.
60. Also known as the Gray-headed Yellow Wagtail. Doubleday's letter was dated December 29th 1834, and the incident was also recorded by him in Loudon's *Mag. nat. Hist.*, 1835, Vol. VIII, p.194. This bird was also kept in his own collection and sold, together with five other birds, for 34 shillings in 1871. On March 13th 1873 he contributed a letter on Wagtails to the *Zool.* (1873, VIII) in which he expressed the view that Gilbert White of Selborne had confounded the Yellow with the Gray Wagtail, pointing out that the adult Gray is yellow underneath, hence Gilbert White's confusion.
61. 1836, *A Nomenclature of British Birds*, published by Westley & Davis. Critical notices were received in various publications including Neville Wood's *Naturalist*, II, 1837. It is possible that the Rev. F. O. Morris may have been a little put out by Doubleday who in the Preface to his *Nomenclature* referred to 'a recent List' which, he said, contained many typographical errors, six species with no claim to be British, five species given twice and twenty-seven unquestioned British birds omitted. Morris' List was dated October 1834 and Doubleday may well have had this in mind.
Edward Newman asked Doubleday for two copies of his '*List of Birds*', in a letter dated October 3rd 1838, which were wanted by Longmans. (Essex Field Club Library).
62. Yarrell's book *British Birds* was started in 1835, and the 3rd and last volume completed in 1843, the 2nd edition published in 1845, and 3rd in 1856, which was the year of his death, and the 4th between 1871 and 1885. His book on Fishes which was completed in 1836 ran through several editions, but had not the scientific popularity of the Birds. William Yarrell (1784–1856) was born at Bayford in Hertfordshire, his mother's native village; he was the last survivor of 12 brothers and sisters all of whom, with his parents, were buried at Bayford.
63. This specimen of American Scaup is referred to in the *Zool.* 1847, V, p.1778, in the article entitled '*Description of and Notes respecting Paget's Pochard, a new species of the Duck Tribe*', by William R. Fisher, F.L.S.; in it he

mentions that only three examples of this rare bird had been recorded, of the other two, one being in the possession of Mr. Gurney and the other, also bought in a London market was Mr. Bartlett's. They were all three later exhibited together by Bartlett at a meeting of the Zoological Society, when the name *Fuligula ferinoides* was suggested (1856, *Zool*. XIV).

64. The date when the young Two-barred Crossbill was shot is not disclosed, but as it is not mentioned in the 1st edition of Yarrell's book, it was probably between 1843 (the date of issue of the second volume) and 1856 when the second supplement was issued, and the bird mentioned, as it was in the later editions. Miller Christy was unable to trace any reference to the bird in the letters to Heysham. This species, which Miller Christy mentioned was so rare that two specimens only had been recorded from Essex (1890, *Birds of Essex*) was referred to by Yarrell in his earlier edition as *Loxia falcirostra*, but later adopted the more generally accepted *L. bifasciata*.

As mentioned in the text, the first Common Crossbill seen by Doubleday was in 1833, when he shot an adult male in 'coppery-green' plumage, of which, when he reported to Heysham, he wrote 'It is the only one I ever saw here, and was evidently a very old bird from the toughness of the fibres etc'. He wrote about two years later 'A small number of Crossbills came here about the middle of August (1835) but remained only a few days. I shot three or four and have one alive.' In that year, and the following one, it was, however, abundant in the Saffron Walden district of Essex, and this rare and irregular Essex visitor, which does occasionally arrive in large numbers, was common at Epping in 1838 and 1839, when it certainly bred there. Doubleday made careful studies of this bird in its years of abundance, writing many informative letters, such as the one to Heysham of November 7th 1838:—

'About the middle of July we were visited by hundreds of Crossbills, but at that time the plumage was so bad they were not worth preserving. Many of them were nestlings. Some yet remain, and I killed four very fine ones in our garden a few days since. I have taken infinite pains to ascertain the changes of plumage and have sent a long history to Yarrell. One thing is certain: that some young males at least become *yellow* at the first autumnal moult. Two males I killed a few days since, one is bright clear yellow, the other fine light red. A bird I have alive has just moulted. He was very red: now he is quite yellow. They are very puzzling.'

The next year, 1839, in a letter written in June, he gave a description of the nest and eggs. Of the latter he remarked:—
'The eggs also strikingly resemble those of the Greenfinch, but are rather larger. Hewitson's figure is very bad. I should hardly think it was a Crossbill's egg from which it was taken.'

On the 3rd May 1840, he wrote:—
'On Tuesday last, as I was walking in our garden, I was surprised to hear the call of the Crossbill, not having seen or heard one for nearly a year. I soon saw five of them flying over, and wanting a pair of them for a friend, I shot at them and killed a male and a female. I regretted afterwards that I did so, as the female was evidently sitting, from the state of her breast.'

A. G. More, in his paper '*On the distribution of Birds in Great Britain during the Nesting season*' in *Ibis* (1865 p. 131 et seq), and Harting in his *Handbook of British Birds* (1872, p.29 et seq) carry the records of Doubleday's observations on these birds for Epping. Newman in the *Zool*. for 1848 acknowledged his help 'in preparing a list of Godalming (where Newman lived) birds as part of the appendix to his *Letters of Rusticus*.'

65. *Zool.* 1873 VIII, Memoir of Dix by Henry Stevenson. The male bird was obtained from Thetford, and the female from Carlisle.
66. *Ibid.* 1861 XIX.
67. *Ibid.* 1875 X.
68. In rough chronological order, a few of Doubleday's remarks follow. In a letter to Heysham dated August 1831, he wrote of the Grosbeak, which 'I believe breeds in our extensive forest every year and I doubt not I can procure thee specimens in November, as at that time it draws near gardens and plantations to feed on the stones of the plum, cherry, laurel etc. It is an extremely shy bird and difficult to shoot, as it darts with great rapidity through the laurels, firs etc., and seldom shows itself till out of reach of shot'.
Of the Whinchat he remarked, in November 1831, on the large numbers seen in Epping Forest, but some years later, in September 1839 he commented that the bird 'has been so remarkably scarce here this year that I do not think I have seen half-a-dozen all round this neighbourhood.' He again remarked on its extreme rarity 'over the last few years' in a letter of May 1843. He commented in a letter of 1832 that he had seen a snow-white specimen in a Colchester collection, which had been obtained locally.
In November 1831 he confirmed also the fluctuation in numbers of the closely related Stonechat in the Forest area, observing that it had totally disappeared in the last three years, whereas formerly it abounded on the furze bushes bordering the Forest. He confirmed its absence when in 1833 he again wrote that he had not seen a single specimen for three years.
The Ring Ouzel is a bird, which although rarely breeding in Essex, is just occasionally seen as a migrant, and sufficiently scarce for Doubleday to refer to on a number of occasions: in October 1832 for example he shot a young male in Epping which had a very indistinct ring, and others in the Forest some years later: one frequented his garden at Epping in November 1871, where he saw it feeding on the haws of a red thorn, and on yew berries, and ever on the alert for wild life he noted one feeding on a haw-bush 'as I was riding to Chelmsford yesterday': this was written on 21st October 1836.
The Lesser Redpoll (*Linota rufescens*), a resident in Scotland and the north of England regularly visits Essex in winter, and occasionally breeds there: he wrote of their early arrival in 1840 'I do not know whether we are likely to have a sharp winter or not, but I see some birds from the north are arriving. I have seen flocks of Redpolls for three weeks past. We do not often see them so early here'—in a letter of September 24th.
A pair of Mealy Redpolls (*L. linaria*) were sent alive to Doubleday from Colchester in January 1836, and he supplied specimens of this bird to Yarrell; he certainly kept them alive in his aviary at Epping for a time. A male of this species, also known as the Stone Redpoll, which is in Saffron Walden Museum, was killed in that town in 1836. It is much rarer than the Lesser Redpoll. Many of Doubleday's birds found their way into collections of considerable scientific value, yet we must not overlook the fact that many were also distributed to friends living in country houses, perhaps a long way from Epping: Harry Blake Knox of Dublin for example received a case of Mealy Redpolls from him to which he referred in his article on '*Ornithological Notes from the County of Dublin for 1867*' in *Zool.* III 1868. It was fashionable at that time to display cases of our native birds, but we cannot help rejoicing that, although Doubleday was an excellent shot the bird sometimes eluded his gun, as did the Stone Redpoll in January 1836: writing from Epping he related:—'I have never yet met with one in this vicinity but about three weeks since I had the pleasure of seeing it wild,

feeding on the alder, in company with a number of Siskins, near Colchester. I shot one and immediately after a specimen with a fine rose-coloured breast alighted on the alder close to me, but flew ere I could load my gun. I cannot see that any of the bird-catchers have ever taken the Stone Redpoll here.' Saffron Walden Museum also received a gift of a pair of Wood Larks from Doubleday: in the early 1830's it was a rare resident in Epping Forest, but in 1839 and 1840 he said they were increasing 'but I fear the London bird-catchers will thin them'. In 1880, James English, Henry Doubleday's life-long assistant, included it in his list of resident Epping birds.

Miller Christy in his *Birds of Essex* remarked that the Lesser Whitethroat, a summer visitor to Essex, was rarer than the Common Whitethroat, although Doubleday, in 1831, remarked that the Lesser was 'equally common with the larger one, and much more destructive to fruit in gardens. Its song is very different from any other bird's'.

As was to be expected, the birds which received much of Doubleday's attention were those of the woodlands, which were so close to his home, but although the Green Woodpecker was particularly common in the Epping area, the Lesser Spotted Woodpecker, whilst included in his brother Edward's, and English's list of Epping birds, was rarely seen—'I have seen it here once or twice' he wrote in 1832, and later, in 1840 'It is, as far as my observation goes, very rare . . . a solitary struggling individual or two, is all I ever heard of anywhere round us.' Similarly, he had never seen the nest of the Pied or Great Spotted Woodpecker until 1832, which confirmed its rarity.

A specimen of the locally distributed Wood Wren (another name for the Wood Warbler) which 'always frequents woods, generally where there are tall trees' he wrote in the *Zool.*, was also given to Saffron Walden Museum. Miller Christy knew of only two localities, Epping and Saffron Walden, where this uncommon summer visitor had been seen in Essex.

In 1832 'the Forest literally swarms with them' he wrote of the Redstart, and it was of this bird that Miller Christy related in his book the following anecdote:—'After the excavations in 1878 at the site of the supposed Saxon cemetery in the grounds of the late Mr. George Stacey Gibson at Saffron Walden when nearly two hundred skeletons were discovered, a Redstart made its nest and reared four young in one of the skulls during the time it remained exposed. Access to the interior was obtained through the eye orbit. The skull and nest, which I have seen, are still in the possession of Mrs. Gibson.' It is believed they were subsequently presented to the Saffron Walden Museum, which her father-in-law, Jabez Gibson (1794–1838) helped to found in 1832; an account of a visit to the Museum was published in the *Essex Literary Journal* in 1838, and the story of its foundation appeared in the *Essex Rev.* XLI, 1932.

Some assistance to George Stacey Gibson was given by Henry Doubleday, who provided him with a list of plants found in the Epping district for inclusion in his '*Flora of Essex*' published in 1862. Gibson, whose death in 1883 created a wide gap in Saffron Walden affairs was greatly respected, and on the afternoon of his funeral, in the words of the *Herts and Essex Observer*, the county paper, 'every shop in the place was closed, and the shutters put up, and in every private house were the blinds drawn down. Then the populace flocked into the High Street by hundreds.' He was a banker and botanist who passed on much of his local botanical knowledge to Edward Forster of Leytonstone, to be incorporated in a *Flora of Essex*, but when no manuscript came to light upon Forster's death in 1849, Gibson undertook the work, which he so successfully completed (*Essex Rev.* XVI, 1907).

The Rev. C. B. Abdy bought a Bittern at Doubleday's sale in 1871, which was shot at Coopersale near Epping; this bird, which was believed by Miller Christy to be the last Epping specimen, was originally in the possession of the Rev. J. W. Maitland of Loughton, and was probably the one referred to by Doubleday in a letter of January 19th 1832 'A fine Bittern was shot here yesterday—a singular place for such a bird.' A singular place also was Passingford Bridge, about five miles from Epping, for the shooting of a Little Bittern by a man employed by a miller, Mr. Stevens. This bird, young and in beautiful plumage passed into the hands of Sir C. C. Smith of Sutton, said Glegg in *Birds of Essex*, 1890. Doubleday recorded in the *Zool.* IX, 1874, the shooting of this rare bird.

He also wrote to Heysham on the Fieldfare, of which he 'saw vast flocks on the 10th and 11th of May'; this letter was written in July 1834, thus supporting the contention that Doubleday undoubtedly kept a diary which has never come to light. It was reported also that an albino Swallow, entirely without trace of colouring, was observed by Doubleday flying over his garden at Epping on 19th August 1855.

'On calm moonlight evenings in spring we frequently hear the call of this interesting bird' Edward Doubleday wrote of the Stone Curlew in the *Entomological Magazine* in 1835, 'as it passes over at a considerable height. I never knew of more than one specimen being killed in this parish.' In spite of the implication that not only Edward but also his brother Henry identified the cry of this night-time traveller, Miller Christy was rather sceptical of Edward's claim, thinking that perhaps the curious nocturnal call of the Moorhen was mistaken for the cry of the Stone Curlew—unlikely however, as Henry, writing to Heysham mentioned some which flew over Epping in mid-March 1841.

Among the other birds upon which he made interesting observations in communications to the *Zool.* were the Grasshopper Warbler (VIII, 1873), Greater (or Great) Tit, the Cole, Blue and Marsh Tits (II, (O.S.) 1844, and V, 1870), Cuckoo (VIII, 1873), the Chaffinch (IV, 1869) in which he explained the various plumage changes throughout the year, Tree Sparrow (I, (O.S.) 1843) and (IX, 1874), Redwing (1864) and Barn Owl (1843 and 1864). In 1858 the Editor, Edward Newman, described Doubleday, Bond, Salmon and Wolley as 'par excellence the British ornithologists' when inviting the four naturalists to give opinions on the identity of certain species of Grouse, a problem raised by G. Norman in that magazine.

The Woodcock, which is but rarely seen in Epping Forest was first reported by Henry Doubleday as nesting there in April 1844 (W. E. Glegg, *Birds of Essex*, 1890).

69. There is another reference to Doubleday travelling outside the mainland of England, and that occurs in an article dated 17th December 1874 which appeared in the *Ent.* in 1875 (VIII, p.29 et seq) written by W. A. Luff entitled '*Additions to the List of Macrolepidoptera inhabiting Guernsey and Sark*', and of one insect, *Dianthoecia conspersa*, he says Doubleday informed him that he took specimens in Sark more than 20 years previously; lack of opportunity, however, makes this event unlikely, and no confirmation of it has been obtained elsewhere. Doubleday may not have seen this report, published in the year of his death. Incidentally, correspondence took place in the *Ent.* for 1873 (Vol. VI) regarding this moth, and *D. compta*, the larvae of which were common on garden pinks in the neighbourhood of Paris, said Doubleday.

70. Among those for which he had high praise was that of M. Pierret (*Zool.* I, 1843).

71. Guenée certainly received entomologists at his home; Doubleday's friend Stainton reported on a visit to him at Châteaudun when writing from Paris in 1857 (*Entomologist's Weekly Intelligencer*, 1857 No. 31).

72. So wrote a contemporary essayist Joseph Woods, F.L.S. in the *Phytol.* (O.S.) II, 1843 (No. XXXI, p.784) '*Botanical Excursion to France in the summer of* 1843'.

73. Vide *Zool.* XV, 1857 (Letter 14.11.1856). *Callunae* was then unknown, both Doubleday and his visitor pronouncing the larvae to be of an unrecorded species. In an earlier contact with Weaver, Doubleday expressed himself in a rather forthright manner when the former announced with great joy that a larva had produced a fine female moth which he thought was *Clostera anachoreta* (*Zool.* X, 1852. Letter 17.2.1852). This insect, rarely found here, and a doubtful British species, was examined by Doubleday, who commented some months later (*Zool.* X 1852. Letter Nov. 1852) 'I have seen the specimen of *anachoreta*, recorded by Mr. Weaver, and find it is nothing but the common *reclusa*. It does not differ in the least from the ordinary appearance of the species except in perhaps, being a little more ferruginous. If I had bred it, I should have thought nothing of it!'

74. Gaze contributed '*Lepidoptera in Suffolk*' to the *Zool.* I, (O.S.) 1843, and was the author of the article on the Swallowtail Butterfly in Newman's *British Butterflies*. He was also mentioned by Stainton in the *Entomologist's Weekly Intelligencer* (1857 No. 33) as the captor of the rare *lathonia* (Queen of Spain Fritillary) in a lane near Lavenham in Suffolk.

75. Bombyx populeti (L). J. C. Fabricius. *Syst. Ent.* 1775.

76. *Zool.* II, 1844. But this migratory insect is usually scarce, some years not having been recorded at all.

77. It was of this butterfly that Doubleday recorded an extremely early appearance in 1841, on June 18th. This date was mentioned by J. C. Dale as the earliest record in his '*Earliest and latest dates of the appearance of some of the rarer British Butterflies*', in *Ent.* 1872.

78. *Zool.* V, 1847 pp. 1912–3.

79. The *Catalogue* appeared in four parts, the dates of which are marked on the copy presented by H. T. Stainton to the Entomological Society in 1850. (vide *J. Soc. Bibl. nat. Hist.* 1937, Vol. I Pt. 3 p. 87).

80. Feb. 1832.

81. Newman included four moths in this family—the Short-cloaked Moth, and the Least, Small, and Scarce, Black Arches Moths.

82. *Ent.* V, 1870/1, pp.33–43.

83. *Zool.* IX, 1851.

84. *Ibid.* XIV, 1856.

85. *Ent.* V, 1870/1.

86. *Zool.* VII (2nd ser.) 1872.

87. It was not only the lepidopterists who came in for such criticism, but also the coleopterists; G. R. Crotch for example was severely dealt with by E. C. Rye for having the 'idea of establishing the Continental System among us.'

88. An informative article on the Club was published in *Zool.* XV, 1857. The collections, which were considerably augmented by Doubleday, and the library, were at certain times open to inspection by members.

89. *Zool.* XIX, 1861.

90. J. W. Douglas. *Entomological Localities—Box Hill, Surrey, and its vicinity.* 'Many a time seated on the verdant turf, under a wide-spreading tree, have his varied knowledge and classic lore shed a new charm over the beautiful scenes around.' (*Zool.* 1852, Vol. X, p.3343 et seq.).

91. This Expedition, sponsored also by Sir Fowell Buxton, was a brave but perhaps misguided attempt to introduce European civilisation to West Africa; three ships took part, fever breaking out in all of them, and although one, the Albert, penetrated 300 miles up the Niger, it was impossible, in view of the toll of lives, to proceed further. Buxton, to whom the project was very dear to his heart, was sorely hurt by the disaster, and died within a few years.

92. The Royal Society enumerated 29 of his papers in its *Catalogue of Scientific Papers*, and Agassiz in the Ray Society's *Bibliographia Zoologicae* found 25 worthy of mention, and the specific name *Doubledayi* is mentioned in connection with nine species of butterflies named after Edward Doubleday in Kirby's '*A synonymic List of diurnal Lepidoptera*' (1872). '*On the Genera of Diurnal Lepidoptera*' was issued in monthly parts at five shillings each part, the first being published in November 1846, and it was intended that two coloured plates should be included in each part of which the total number was to be not more than 40.

93. *Travels in New Zealand* II, 1843, London. The collective list of the known insects of New Zealand in this book was compiled by Adam White and Edward Doubleday.

94. In two parts, Part I in 1844, Part II in 1847.

95. Vol. I, 2me Serie.

96. After Edward Doubleday's death his portrait by Maguire was presented to the Entomological Society by George Ransome, and copies could be obtained for the modest sum of five shillings; a memoir of his life was read to the Society by Mr. Douglas, Edward Doubleday's coadjutor. (*Zool.* VIII, 1850).

97. Lawson was born at Settle, entered Christ's College, Cambridge in 1650, and was appointed minister of Rampside parish in Lancashire: it was when he was there that George Fox, the dynamic founder of the Quakers, visited the town, and an account of the historic meeting with Lawson appears in Fox's *Diary*. Lawson resigned his living, and joined the Quakers, subsequently suffering great persecution.

98. John Coakley Lettsom (1744–1812) a doctor, and Lewis Weston Dillwyn, a pottery manufacturer, were also eminent botanists, and members of the Royal Society. An account of these and many others may be found in Arthur Raistrick's *Quakers in Science and Industry* (1950) in which the author clearly shows the climate in which these men were nurtured, 'In the realms of medicine and science it would almost seem that the pioneering spirit found the easiest expression. The complete break from dependence upon an established authority in matters spiritual, coupled with the Quaker insistence on the unity of life, an insistence which seemed to be instinctive and almost involuntary, produced the ideal mental attitude for the scientist.' Other early Quaker botanists included Collinson, Miller, Bartram, Fothergill and Curtis. Peter Collinson (1693–1768), who corresponded with Linnaeus and doubtless met him when the latter visited London in 1736, introduced many new plants, shrubs and trees from abroad. Phillip Miller (1691–1771), whose herbarium is now in the British Museum, and who

also corresponded with Linnaeus, was a member of the Council of the Royal Society. John Bartram (1699–1777) laid the foundation of our knowledge of American flora. John Fothergill (1712–1780) was a doctor for whom botanists in every corner of the world collected, and who amassed a vast collection of rare plants which he cultivated in his garden of 30 acres at Upton in Essex, now the site of the Park at West Ham. William Curtis, (1746–1799) perhaps the best known of all, started the *Botanical Magazine* in 1787, ten years after he had commenced publication of *Flora Londinensis*; and his rare pamphlet '*History of the Brown-tail Moth*' is well known.

99. A great deal of controversy raged in the early volumes of Newman's protégé, the *Phytologist* (Vol. I (O.S.) 1841, II (O.S.) 1844, III (O.S.) 1848) and was discussed in the *Gardener's Chronicle* (1867) and elsewhere. Darwin debated the species in the *Journal of Proc. Linn. Soc.* (VI, 1862, X 1868).

100. Darwin, C., 1877, *The different forms of flowers on plants of the same species*. Murray.

101. '*On the species of the genus Primula in Essex*', Essex Field Club *Trans. and Proc.* III, 1883/4.

102. At the great National Fisheries Exhibition at Norwich in 1881, English was awarded a Diploma of Honour for his collection of preserved fungi, which consisted of 39 species, many very rare and interesting: prior to the exhibition he showed the case to members of the Essex Field Club, at a meeting on March 26th 1881. The following year he wrote and published '*A Manual for the preservation of the Larger Fungi in their natural condition, also a new process for the preservation of Wild Flowers, discovered by J. L. English*'. (Printed by Alfred B. Davis, High Street, Epping, 1882, Price 2/6d). English acquired an extraordinarily good knowledge of fungi, gained from his own practical experience, and a great deal of information about their habitats and peculiarities was known to him alone. Naturally enough, he was soon recognised as the fungus expert of the Essex Field Club, of which he acted, so long as his health lasted, as Conductor at their Annual Fungus Forays, still a yearly event in their calendar; and the first prizes at the Fungus Shows of the Royal Horticultural Society usually fell to English's collection, so skilful did he become at gathering them. The lists of lepidoptera, fungi and mosses in E. N. Buxton's *Epping Forest* (1884) were contributed by him. See also *Trans. and Proc.* of *Essex Field Club* II 1881/2, IV 1885/6.

103. *Essex Nat.* 1900, XI.

104. *Phyt.* I (O.S.) 1841.

105. *Ibid.* I (O.S.) 1842. Letter from Henry Doubleday, 14th June 1842.

106. *Ibid.* II (O.S.) 1843.

107. *Zool.* XVI, 1858.

108. *Ibid.* XV, 1858.

109. *Ibid.* XIX, 1861.

110. Among the other species of this attractive little family of moths the *Eupitheciae*, carefully examined by Doubleday, were Guenée's Pug, *E. pernotata*, identified by Guenée from a moth bred by Doubleday from larvae feeding on golden-rod, collected by Mr. Machin. (*Zool.* XV, 1858); *E. pulchellata* which because of its similarity with *E. linariata*, had confused many entomologists for a long time who thought they were not distinct species, but Doubleday found the food plant of *pulchellata* and proved they were distinct by breeding them both simultaneously (even Guenée, who was doubtful, was persuaded by this proof. (*Zool.* XXII, 1864)). Others were *E. fraxinata*,

E. innotata and *E. minutata*, which were the subject of his correspondence in *Entomologist* and *Zoologist*.

About two months before his death in 1875 he described fully in the *Entomologist* the very rare and striking moth *E. extensaria* of Freyer, which he had identified for Mr. Sawyer of Hull, who had found it on waste ground. 'Dr. Staudinger has never had it for sale' said Doubleday, who had been given two specimens, a male and female, but in poor condition, by Julius Lederer, who confirmed its scarcity: in fact, said Doubleday, it had never before been found outside Russia: this insect could possibly have been imported in a cargo ship. *E. haworthiata*, Haworth's Pug, was given this name by Doubleday who first realised that the variety characterised by our outstanding descriptive entomologist, Haworth, was a separate species; unfortunately Doubleday did not know that Treitschke had earlier described and named it *E. isogrammata*, which name, in accordance with priority rules, had to be retained.

111. *Zool.* IV, 1846.

112. Newman, in *British Moths* (1869), quotes Doubleday in connection with others of this family, e.g. *lutarella, stramineola, griseola.*

113. *Zool.* V, 1847.

114. *Ibid.* XIX, 1861.

115. *caniola* was exhibited by Mr. Bond in the autumn of 1861 at a meeting of the Entomological Society in London.

116. In due course a translation by Newman of Guenée's monograph on the genus *Lithosia* from *Annales de la Société Entomologique de France*, 1861 appeared in *Zool.* (XXI, 1863) and in it all the British representatives of the family are described, Guenée acknowledging his debt to his friend Doubleday for the loan of his specimens. Guenée named a new species *Lithosia molybdeola*, and some controversy was instigated by the Reverend Joseph Greene who queried whether it had been described and named as *L. sericea* by the entomologist C. S. Gregson. Greene felt this was the case, and wrote:— 'If *sericea* be the first name given to this species I for one shall certainly use it, as I think it at least as good as the other, besides being an English insect and named by an English entomologist.' *Zool.* XXI, 1863. Our friend Doubleday wrote in reply a rather lengthy but spirited and reasoned letter to the *Zoologist* in which he took the view that it was common knowledge that Guenée was preparing his monograph, therefore this rare insect should not have been named by Gregson; other well-known entomologists agreed, including Professor Westwood and Major Parry. In concluding this controversy, the editor, Newman, wrote:—'I beg this subject may now be dropped; it is evident that my friend Mr. Doubleday has never had any selfish feeling with regard to Entomology, but has always done everything in his power to assist his fellow labourers in the science. It may be thought by most of my readers that there was no necessity for even this reply on his part, but to me it seems that a feeling of courtesy to Mr. Greene demands the explanation Mr. Doubleday has now given. I may add that I entirely and heartily concur in the spirit of the passages Mr. Doubleday has cited from Major Parry and Professor Westwood, and I should decline to enter into the question whether the description of M. Guenée or Mr. Gregson were the first printed. Mr. Gregson will, I trust, kindly accept these lines as an intimation that I respectfully decline his rather voluminous paper on the same subject.'

Many of the *Lithosia* were given to Doubleday by a collector named Greening, who was of great help both to Doubleday and Guenée in their efforts to determine species, and in one letter to Doubleday Greening said:—'It is always a pleasure to me to assist anyone working out the history of an insect, and especially you, who have so often assisted me.'

117. *Ent.* VI, 1873. In *Zool.* XIX, 1861 some correspondence took place over a specimen of this family taken in Ireland by Mr. Birchall; it was referred to Doubleday who as usual consulted Guenée, whose letter was quoted verbatim in the *Zool.* by Doubleday. The confusion arose because of the resemblance between *Z. achilleae* (the Oban Burnet) and *Z. minos,* and the moth, pronounced by Guenée, (referred to by Newman on this occasion as 'that greatest of Lepidopterists') as a new species, was named by Newman *Z. nubigena.*

118. *Z. exulans* is known here as the Mountain Burnet—a very rare and local moth.

119. *Ent.* VI, 1873.

120. *Zool.* III, 1845.

121. Newman. *British Moths* 1869.

122. C. Nicholson, *Rosy Marbled Moth in Britain,* Essex Nat. 1922, XX.

123. Firmin, Pyman *et al* 1975 *A guide to the Butterflies and Larger Moths of Essex.*

124. *Ent.* I 1840. The third specimen was shown by Rev. J. Greene at the Meeting of the Entomological Society of London, in 1854.

125. Doubleday gave reasons why he thought the Brimstone could not be bivoltine, saying 'I have reared numbers from the eggs, and can speak positively on the subject'; his chief opponent on that occasion was his long standing friend H. T. Stainton, who somewhat ill-advisedly wrote to the *Zoologist* 'and yet no entomologist exists in Britain sufficiently observant to have noticed the transformation of *G. rhamni,* the double-broodedness of which was never questioned till the Editor of the *Zoologist* thought he had discovered a mare's nest.' The letter of protest which followed from Edwin Shepherd put the point that 'Mr. Stainton's enquiries are in effect already answered by the excellent remarks of my friends Doubleday and Douglas'. Doubleday too challenged Stainton's remarks, calling them a libel upon his fellow labourers in science. 'That some persons who profess to have a thorough knowledge of the transformations of the minute tribes are profoundly ignorant of the economy of the larger lepidoptera, I can readily believe, but *all* have not begun at the wrong end.' That Doubleday's equable temper should have been so ruffled is surprising, especially as his criticism was undoubtedly aimed at Stainton, the first volume of whose book, *Natural History of Tineina* was published in that year (1855).

126. *Depressariae*—tiny moths known as the 'flat-bodies.'

127. *Zool.* XIV 1856.

128. G. R. Crotch took an unidentified Wainscot in 1861, which Doubleday sent to Guenée to determine, who pronounced it *Nonagria elymi* of Treitschke: the first specimen caught in England, however, was captured by Mr. Winter 'who preceded Crotch by three or four minutes'! (*Zool.* XIX 1861). *Leucania loreyi* (Duponchel) has been captured on several occasions at Brighton, which curious circumstance caused Doubleday to write to the *Zoologist* (XXI, 1863) as follows:—
'The fact that nearly all the species of Lepidoptera recently discovered in the South of England are natives of the Southern portion of Europe, and

111

are never found on the Northern coast, renders it very improbable that these specimens are of Continental origin. In a letter recently received from Dr. Staudinger, he remarks upon the singularity of our country which produces so many Southern forms.'
Whether Doubleday's suspicion was aroused by these captures is not known: certainly he was only too well aware of the unscrupulous methods employed by many dealers, so it would appear that he was satisfied as to their authenticity, as he must have been when some years later, in August 1873. G. Parry of Canterbury took a pair of *Leucania* near Romney Marsh, which he could not place: he sent them to Doubleday, who returned them to Parry on 3rd September 1873 giving his opinion that they were identical with a moth taken by his brother Edward Doubleday many years before in the State of New York, and which he had sent to Guenée to describe and name, which he did, identifying it as *commoïdes*. Newman gave Guenée's description in the *Entomologist* in the same year. A specimen of the White-speck or American Wainscot (the American 'Army-worm') was received by Doubleday from a son of Dr. Parker of Lyndhurst early in 1875; he informed Newman (*Ent.* VIII, 1875) of the capture of this insect, which swarms from Canada to Brazil, but is extremely rare in this country.

129. *Zool.* VIII, 1850.

130. *Ibid.* VI, 1848.

131. Thomas Henry Allis, died at York in 1870, aged 53: he was a Quaker, the son of Thomas Allis F.L.S. who survived him. T. H. Allis carried on with the insect collection started by his father.

132. *Ent.* II, 1865.

133. *Ibid*, VIII, 1875.

134. *Zool.* V, 1847.

135. *Ent.* II, 1865.

136. The first description of *Luperina gueneei* was given by Doubleday in the *Entomologist's Annual* for 1864, and then published in the *Entomologist* in the same year.

137. A description of *ashworthii* by Doubleday was read at a meeting of the Entomological Society in London in 1854 (*Zool.* XIII, 1855), and Stevens exhibited larvae at another Entomological Society meeting in November 1856 (*Zool.* XV, 1857).

138. *barrettii* was described by Doubleday in full in Stainton's *Entomologist's Annual* for 1864, and in *Zool.* (XXII) for the same year. The *Entomologist* for 1885 also carried a comprehensive account of the moth.

139. This was reported in *Zool.* XIX, 1861. A few years later Gregson, the northern entomologist, gave his opinion that it was a dark variety of *D. carpophaga* but other entomologists did not agree, especially after Barrett disclosed that in the autumn of 1861, knowing that Doubleday was making up a box of rare British lepidoptera to send to Dr. Herrich-Schäffer, he sent a specimen to Doubleday to enclose; Herrich-Schäffer also identified it as *capsophila* (*Zool.* XXI, 1863). *D. nisus* was another moth, among many, which Doubleday identified for Barrett.

140. *Ent.* VI, 1872/3.

141. *Ibid.* V, 1891 (Paper by Fitch was read Dec. 2nd, 1890).

142. *Proc. Essex Field Club* II, 1881/2.

143. *Ent.* XXII, 1930.

144. *Zool.* XIII, 1855.

145. Letter from Doubleday read by Mr. M'Lachlan at the meeting of the Entomological Society on January 7th, 1867.

146. F. Edward Hulme, *Butterflies and Moths*, (n.d.).

147. *Ent.* VI, 1872/3. A larva of the Scarlet Tiger Moth found at Dover in 1872 produced a melanic form which Mr. Stevens lent Newman for illustration and description in the *Entomologist*: Newman remarked that Doubleday had a similar fine melanic variety in his cabinet.

148. *Ibid.* VI, 1872/3.

149. *Zool.* II (O.S.) 1845.

150. E. Newman, *Natural History of British Moths* 1869.

151. Doubleday bred from larvae collected or received from Whittlesea Mere in Cambridgeshire, many of which he gave away: Thomas Ingall, for example, whose specimens have in the main found a home in the British Museum (Natural History) received a caterpillar from him in June 1841, which he bred into a fine male *dispar*. [Riley, 1927, *Nat. Hist. Mag.* I, 2. (Trustees of the B.M.)].

152. *Essex Nat.* I, 1887.

153. *V. C. H. Essex* I, 1903.

154. *Ibid.*

155. *Phigalia*—generic name for a few species of moths known as 'Brindled Beauties'.

156. *Ent.* VI, 1873.

157. *Zool.* XV, 1857.

158. *Ent.* II, 1864/5.

159. *Zool.* IV, 1846.

160. *Ent. mon. Mag.* IX, 1872/3.

161. A. W. Mera 1925. *Increase in melanism in the last half-century. Lond. Nat.*

162. *Vide* Dr. H. B. D. Kettlewell, 1958, *Heredity* XII, Pt. I.

163. *Ent. mon. Mag.* IX, 1872/3.

164. Edward Doubleday 1848, *Ann. Mag. Nat. Hist.* I.

165. Darwin 1845, *Naturalist's Voyage.*

166. *Zool.* III, 1868.

167. *Vide* letter on *Cucullia* genus. *Zool.* VII, 1849.

168. Newman 1869, *Natural History of British Moths.*

169. *Trans. and Proc. Essex Field Club* 1881/2, II.

170. The lecture was given on 30th April 1881.

171. The two specimens of *occulta* which Doubleday caught were a female on 1st August, and a male on 4th August 1842.

172. This record, in the *Dictionary of National Biography*, is not strictly true, as Miller Christy is ignoring the four months which he spent during his illness in the Retreat at York: and in 1873 he spent two days with his old friend W. C. Hewitson at Oatlands. What powers of persuasion must have been employed to entice Doubleday from his beloved Epping!

173. The reference to Edward Doubleday's action in 1832 provides the first
definite link between moths and sugar, as pointed out by P. B. M. Allan
in his entertaining book *Talking of Moths* (1943), and in his 2nd Edition
of *A Moth-Hunter's Gossip* (1947). Allan also mentions evidence of 'sugaring' being practised in Northumberland in 1834 by Selby, of Twizel, who
undoubtedly followed Edward's example: this was brought to the notice
of P. B. M. Allan in a letter to the *Entomologist* (1942, LXXV) dated 6th
December 1941 from Capt. Bacon, after the first publication in 1937 of *A
Moth-Hunter's Gossip*, when Allan was unaware of Edward's letter of 1832.
Although it was clear to everyone that many insects, including lepidoptera,
were attracted by sweetness, and indeed, Abel Ingpen in *Instructions for
Collecting, Rearing and Preserving British Insects*, 1827, says 'A sheet laid
on the ground in a garden or wood in a hot Summer's day will attract many
insects. As sweets will attract them within doors, there is little doubt but
they might be employed to advantage without. Sheets of white paper
smeared with honey water, beer, and sugar, or sugar sprinkled over them
would answer the purpose,' yet the credit for the first *nocturnal* 'sugaring'
should doubtless go to the Doubledays.

Edward Newman, whose close life-long association with Henry has been
demonstrated, certainly had no doubts, for he wrote of 'sugaring' which
'he (Henry) not merely originated, but brought to perfection' in the *Entomologist* (VIII) a few months before Henry died in 1875.

174. He was able to say in 1871 that all the British *Xanthias* (The 'Sallows'),
except *Aurago* (Barred), were taken on these trees; they were *Ferruginea*,
(The Brick), *Silago* (Pink-barred), *Citrago* (Orange), *Cerago* (Sallow) and
the pale variety (the *Gilvago* of Haworth), (Dusky-Lemon). He was particularly pleased to announce the capture of fine male and female specimens
of *Gilvago*, which he did not think had occurred before in the neighbourhood
of London. The species was perhaps not so rare as Doubleday thought,
however, as some had been taken by Horley and others at Hoddesdon,
about 20 miles from London, and once by H. D. Greville at Coombe Wood,
near London, in 1870. (*Ent.* V, 1870/1).

175. 21st April 1875.

176. *V.C.H.* I, 1903.

177. Fitter 1959 *The Ark in our midst.*

178. Pattiswick Hall was owned by Mrs. J. Smith, an aunt of Robert Miller
Christy, who exhibited the bat at a meeting of the Essex Field Club in
February 1883. (*Proc. of Essex Field Club*, IV, 1885-6). This record is a
rather interesting one, as the Serotine, which is one of the largest and most
powerful of our dozen native species, is rarely found north of the Thames.
One specimen had been recorded from Hertfordshire, and two from Glamor-
gan, (Vesey-Fitzgerald, 1949, *British Bats*) but this one from Pattiswick
Hall was probably the first Essex example. Mrs. Smith was the mother of
Miss C. Fell Smith, for many years the editor of the *Essex Review*, and a
keen student of local history and Essex flora and fauna. It is recorded that
Mrs. Smith acquired the herbarium of Thomas Batt Hall with its 184
specimens of mosses and lichens all beautifully mounted on white paper,
which she presented in 1890 to the Essex Field Club. (*Essex Rev.* XXXII,
1923). Hall, who was acquainted with most of the Essex naturalists, including John Brown F.G.S. of Stanway (1780–1859), S. P. Woodward (1821–
1865), Dr. E. G. Varenne of Kelvedon, the Gibsons of Saffron Walden and
the Doubleday brothers, was educated in Coggeshall, and must have known
well the Doubledays in that town: his father, John Hall, was a partner in a

Coggeshall firm of silk-throwsters. T. B. Hall was known for his *Flora of Liverpool* (see *The first Liverpool Flora and its Author*, by A. A. Dallman, and *Lancashire and Cheshire Naturalist* XIV, 6) where he lived for a time before returning to Coggeshall; sadly, it is said that after his marriage he got into difficulties, and later went to Australia.

179. *Essex Nat.* IX, 1895/6.

180. *Zool.* (N.S.) I, 1866.

181. *Ibid.* (N.S.) IV, 1869.

182. *Trans. Essex Field Club* I, 1880.

183. An eye witness account of such an incident is given by Guy Dollman, of the British Museum [1936, *Nat. Hist. Mag.* V, No. 40 (Trustees of the B.M.)].

184. Letters from Loddiges were dated 28.11.1842 and 13.1.1843. A number of letters on the subject of humming birds passed between Doubleday and Loddiges, an authority who contributed a number of papers on them to scientific magazines; Doubleday sent Dix a book on these birds on 4th October 1854, together with a number of bird skins and a pair of Grey Shrikes, the male of which he shot in his field at Epping. A few other letters to Dix are preserved, all in the Essex Field Club Library, which were acquired from the late Miss Maria Dix of Ipswich. In one, dated 9th November 1853, Doubleday gives his recipe for 'arsenical soap', used in his bird stuffing work: it is in beautiful handwriting, showing no sign of weakness, and in the letter he mentions that 'Richard "B" ' sent him a Golden-eye Duck which was shot at Harlow—a bird not usually seen so far from the sea.

Dix was born at Dickleburgh, Norfolk in 1830, the family moving to Essex when he was quite young: he later returned to Norfolk. He was a skilful taxidermist and good ornithologist, contributing many papers to the *Zoologist*, one in particular *The Birds of Pembrokeshire*, being of especial value (*Zool.* I (2nd Ser.) 1866). He died about 1873.

Henry received large boxes of bird skins and insects from North America 'many years ago' he mentioned in a letter dated 3rd March 1873, to the *Entomologist's Monthly Magazine* (IX, 1872/3). These were a most certainly sent by his brother Edward, who spent some time collecting in America; included were many skins of beautiful humming birds, which Doubleday stuffed and were later acquired by Miss Annie Warner, a member of an old Hoddesdon, Hertfordshire, Quaker family, and passed, upon her death, to the Braithwaite family also of Hoddesdon. Loddiges and Doubleday received much benefit from exchange of views on the technique of bird-stuffing.

185. 30th December 1857.

186. Probably Overend Gurney & Co., which failed on 'Black Friday', 1866. (*Essex Rev.* I, 1892).

187. The letters are dated 6th February 1867, 4th July 1867, 9th July 1867, 7th November 1867, 29th January 1868, 1st February 1868, 19th August 1868, 15th September 1868, 26th September 1870, 27th October 1870. On 1st April 1910, J. Hartley Durrant, who had been Lord Walsingham's Private Secretary and Entomological Assistant, was appointed by the British Museum (Natural History) 1st Class Assistant in Zoology and Keeper of the Walsingham Collection, which numbered about 354,000 insects.

188. The moth was taken 1st October 1867. Doubleday announced its capture in *Ent.* V 1870, stating the moth is rare everywhere, but is found principally in Hungary and Russia. It is described and figured in Newman's *Insect*

Hunter's Year Book for 1869 (pub. 1870), and was the first specimen ever identified in the British Isles; it remains in the Doubleday Collection in the British Museum (Natural History), and its identity has since been confirmed as a male *'Xylophasia (Sidemia) zollikoferi ab. internigrata.'*
Some years later when writing to H. T. Stainton from the Retreat, the Mental Hospital at York, he expressed surprise and concern that Baron von Nolcken should be in South America—'I hope he may not suffer from a climate so different from that to which he has been accustomed . . . I have heard that high winds are very prevalent in Bogota which makes the collection of lepidoptera rather difficult.'

189. Minute 11 of Monthly Meeting held at Tottenham 9th February 1871 (*Tottenham M.M. Minutes*, 1857–1877, Library of the Society of Friends, London).

190. *Ent*. V, 1870–1 (ex *Petites Nouvelles Entomologiques*).

191. Library of the Society of Friends, London.

192. The 173 lots, in all 540 specimens contained in 288 cases, were sold, realising the sum of £275. A small enough figure when one thinks of the many years of collecting and study which it took to build up the collection. Among the more interesting of the specimens were the first British Blue-headed Wagtail, the White-winged and Parrot Crossbills which were shot at Epping, two Fork-tailed Petrels from Epping and a Bittern from the village of Coopersale, near Epping, which was bought by the Rev. C. B. Abdy.

193. *Ent*. VIII, 1875.

194. The funeral arrangements were carried out by G. J. Lawrence of Epping, the cortège leaving the house of the 'Recluse of Epping' at 11 a.m.

195. *Essex Weekly News*, 9th July 1875.

196. Maull & Polyblank specialised in the portraiture of scientific men, and the firm apparently went to considerable lengths to maintain their pre-eminence in this field; as an example of this may be quoted two paragraphs from a letter written by Robert Brown, the British Museum's first Keeper of the Department of Botany, to Baron von Humboldt in 1857:—
'This note will be delivered to you by Mr. Polyblank, a distinguished Photographer, who has for some time been engaged in taking Portraits of Scientific Men mostly Members of the Linnean Club, and who as well as the Members of that Club is extremely desirous of prefixing yours to that extensive series.
To obtain your kind permission to sit to Him for your Photographic Portrait is his only object in visiting Berlin, and having applied to me for a Letter of introduction I have, I fear, indiscreetly written this Note, which I should not have done had I supposed that the Operation required many minutes of your time.' [1928, *Nat. Hist. Mag.* I, 5. (Trustees of B.M.)].

197. An engraving of Henry's brother Edward was hung there.

198. Joseph Smith, the author, (1819–1896) was for a time resident in Saffron Walden, the 'Quaker town' frequently mentioned in this memoir. (*Essex Rev.* XXIV, 1915).

199. Then a branch of the British Museum (South Kensington).

200. A little later it will be noted that the collections were actually received by the Museum early in 1876; it is not clear therefore what influence the Haggerston Entomological Society had in their bestowal, but on December 2nd 1947, L. G. Payne, in his Presidential Address to the London Natural

History Society (which had developed from the Haggerston Society) stated that 'in 1879 the Society was instrumental in arranging for the Doubleday collection to be presented to the Bethnal Green Museum . . . ' (*London Nat.* 1947, *The Story of our Society.*)

Certain it is that Edward Newman was a prominent member of the Haggerston Entomological Society, his name appearing in the list of 35 at the end of 1858, the year of its birth. It may be mentioned in passing that in the year 1869 Newman presented each member of that Society with a copy of his *Insect Hunter's Year Book*: the number of members had increased considerably (in 1874 there were over 100) and the Society had a considerable library and collection of insects: in the same year Newman presented to the library a copy of his *Natural History of British Moths*.

201. Tompkins' *Companion into Essex* (1938), and the later Addison's *Epping Forest* state that some of Doubleday's collections are 'or were until recently at the Bethnal Green Branch of the South Kensington Museum.' In fact the whole collection was removed from Bethnal Green in 1915.

202. Published by Chapman & Hall 1877.

203. In the old English collections insects were invariably set in English pins and in English fashion—'at that early period' Newman said 'the setting boards which are now so commonly used by beginners and which flatten out the partially folded character of the hind-wings, had not been invented. Few of our English entomologists adopt the old fashion of setting insects with card braces beneath the wings, but Mr. Doubleday is one of them, and his specimens are always distinguishable for the perfectly natural elegance of their shape.' The collection was the neatest and cleanest Newman had ever seen.
A lengthy correspondence in the pages of the *Entomologist* in 1870 and 1871 discussed methods of avoiding grease and preventing attack from mites and Doubleday's views were extensively quoted. The *Zoologist* in 1863 (XXI) also carried correspondence on these subjects referring to Doubleday's practice. By the excellent state of his insects, his methods certainly proved successful.

204. This laudatory verse in Latin forms part of the inscription on the small monument erected to John Ray by his friends, in the churchyard at Black Notley. It was composed by the Rev. William Coyte M.A.
A visit was organised by the Linnaean Club to Ray's tomb on 3rd July 1844. Among those present on that occasion was Edward Newman, who probably took a careful note of the inscription, as several others were known to have done. (Dr. W. Derham, *Select Remains and life of Ray*. Ray Society, 1846). These most appropriate words were also quoted by Dunning in his biographical notice of Doubleday in the *Entomologist*, 1877.

ADDENDA

Whilst the name of the Epping house which was Doubleday's birthplace, was stated to be formerly the Black Boy Inn by many authorities, (including the usually reliable Miller Christy, who contributed the entry on Doubleday in the D.N.B.) and as such is referred to in this memoir, further investigation has shown that much confusion over the name has arisen, and it now seems probable that the correct name, when Joseph Doubleday took it over, was the Black Dog. Evidence supporting this can be found in the *Report of a Special Court Baron* of John Conyers Esquire held on 29th May 1776, in the *Court Rolls* of the Manor of Epping Bury: this refers to the transfer of the Black Dog, otherwise known as Champions, otherwise Broadbents, to Joseph Doubleday. Other references too in the *Epping Court Book* 1791–1803 (E.R.O.) are made to Joseph Doubleday (described at that time as a 'tallowchandler') and the Black Dog.
Frederick Griffiths, a 19th century Epping printer, who published an annual *Almanack*, also thought (1871) it was the Black Dog, and he appeared to be an authority on the local hostelries, but this reference the writer has been unable to verify.
In 1812 Henry Doubleday's father, Benjamin, purchased a ditch and strip of land about 10 feet wide by about 78 feet long 'as divides the North-East side of the Gardens of Benjamin Doubleday from the said Black Lion premises . . . ' (E.R.O. *Epping Court Book* 1804–1814). Perhaps this close association provides an explanation of the discrepancy in the names, for the building whose land adjoined Doubleday's, the Black Lion, (which still stands), was previously known as the Black Boy, until changed in 1755: as far back as 1651 it was known by that name. From all accounts it was an important post-house, open all night, brewing its own ale.

With reference to the linking of Henry Doubleday's name with the earliest record of the capture of moths by 'sugar', in the account within and in Note 173 in the Appendix, an article in the *Entomologist's Record* (1976, 88, No. 1) by Dr. R. S. Wilkinson of Washington, D.C., has caught my attention: in it he discloses that in the Science Museum, Boston, Massachusetts, is a letter from Edward Doubleday to the American entomologist T. W. Harris, which makes it clear that the credit for the idea of 'sugaring' must go to Selby; Edward's brother Henry adopted 'a plan first introduced in a notice by Mr. Selby of Twizel House, Bedford, (*sic*) brushing over the trunks of trees near our house with sugar . . . ' he wrote, on 19th October 1841. 'However,' Wilkinson concludes, 'Henry Doubleday's lustre is little diminished, for the results of his practical application of Selby's idea made the "sugaring" of trees a standard entomological procedure. As for English, the credibility of his assertion is even further lessened.'
This new evidence, which confirms Doubleday's involvement from the earliest conception of the idea, is probably the last word on the subject!